BP PORTRAIT AWARD 2018

National Portrait Gallery

Published in Great Britain by
National Portrait Gallery Publications
National Portrait Gallery
St Martin's Place, London WC2H 0HE

Published to accompany the BP Portrait
Award 2018, held at the National Portrait
Gallery, London, from 14 June to 23
September, Wolverhampton Art Gallery,
from 13 October to 30 November,
Scottish National Portrait Gallery, Edinburgh,
from 15 December to 10 March 2019.

For a complete catalogue of current
publications please visit our website at
www.npg.org.uk/publications

ISBN 978 1 85514 776 8

A catalogue of this book is available
from the British Library.

10 9 8 7 6 5 4 3 2 1

Project Editor: Tijana Todorinovic
Design: Richard Ardagh Studio
Production: Ruth Müller-Wirth
Photography: Prudence Cuming
Printed and bound in Italy
Cover: *Laura* by Shawn McGovern

Every purchase supports the
National Portrait Gallery, London

Supported by BP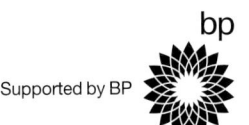

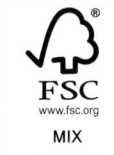

FSC
www.fsc.org

MIX
Paper from
responsible sources
FSC® C016114

CONTENTS

DIRECTOR'S FOREWORD

The BP Portrait Award exhibition is an annual celebration of contemporary painted portraiture by artists of all ages from across the world. The competition from which the exhibited works are drawn is considered the most prestigious in the field of painted portraiture, and continues to attract submissions from the medium's best practitioners. This year 2,667 entries were received from artists in eighty-eight countries. Every painting was carefully assessed in the initial digital judging session in order to arrive at a longlist of just a few hundred for the second round, in which the works are viewed physically, rather than on screen. Over two days of meticulous deliberation we gradually reduced the selection to just forty-eight exceptional portraits for the exhibition.

Judging anonymously requires each panel member to address precisely what they believe makes an outstanding portrait, weighing up the relative importance of technique, likeness, narrative, structure and the overall impact of a work through a lively process of debate and discussion.

This year we congratulate Miriam Escofet for her winning portrait *Angel at my Table*. Our congratulations also go to Felicia Forte and Zhu Tongyao, winners of the second prize and third prize respectively.

At the National Portrait Gallery we are grateful to BP for their sponsorship, now in its 29th year, of the Portrait Award, and for their support of the entire exhibition programme. The provision of the Travel Award has enabled established artists to undertake projects in countries including Burkina Faso, Greece, Japan, Peru and, this year, in Berlin and Mallorca. The winner of this year's Young Artist Award, Ania Hobson, will doubtless provide inspiration for those participating in the BP Next Generation workshops, as they develop their skills. We may even see one of their portraits hanging in the exhibition in a few years' time. Our sincere thanks go to Bob Dudley and his team, and in particular to Dev Sanyal, Peter Mather and Des Violaris for their commitment to the success of this partnership.

Nicholas Cullinan
Director, National Portrait Gallery

SPONSOR'S FOREWORD

Every year the BP Portrait Award helps to inspire thousands of artists to tell a human story using portraiture. The exhibition offers us an insight into the world as seen by the artist, and particularly striking this year is the array of styles on display. Part of the enduring fascination of the competition is that each painting can be interpreted in multiple ways, offering viewers the chance to create their own narratives.

This is the 29th year that BP has supported the award, and the standard is as high as ever. There have been well beyond four million visitors to the exhibitions since we began our partnership with the Gallery. It is pleasing to think that every year thousands of people experience the best in contemporary portraiture from around the world, free of charge.

Since 1990, nearing 38,000 artists have entered the competition. This year more than 2,600 artists from eighty-eight countries submitted entries, with forty-eight selected by the judges for this exhibition. The award offers artists an opportunity to reach a wider audience and in many cases it has been a catalyst

in their artistic career. Our hope at BP is that by supporting this award and other cultural activities in the UK, more people will get the chance to engage with the very best of arts and culture.

As always, we are indebted to the judges for undertaking the challenging process of whittling down the shortlist and selecting the winning works. It is a privilege to work with our partners at the National Portrait Gallery. Dr Nicholas Cullinan, Pim Baxter and their team at the Gallery have put together an exhibition that appeals to a very wide public audience, attracts the admiration of the artistic world, and inspires many to try portraiture themselves. BP looks forward to continuing our support for the award through to 2022.

On behalf of BP, I would like to thank all the artists who submitted work this year and congratulate those who have been selected for the exhibition and shortlisted for the awards.

I hope visitors will enjoy viewing these works as much as I have.

Bob Dudley
Group Chief Executive, BP

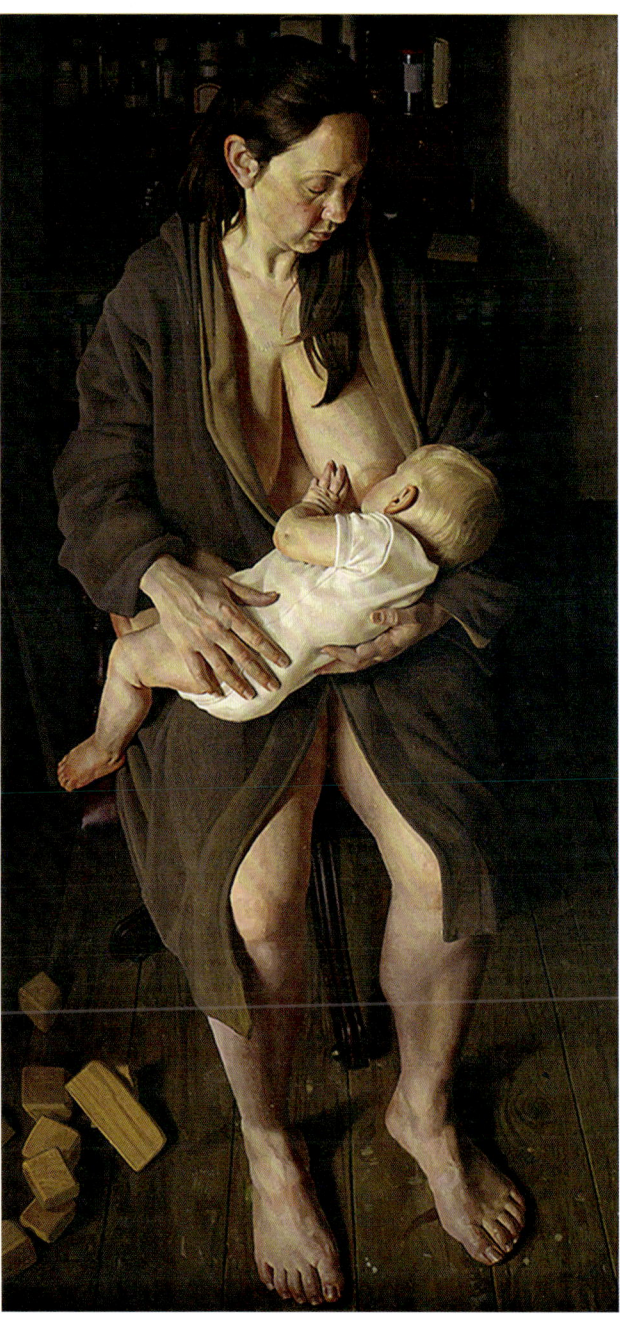

LIVING AND REAL

Rosie Broadley

Curator, Nineteenth-
Century Collections,
National Portrait Gallery

In a letter written in 1880, French artist Édouard Manet lamented the struggle involved in making a successful portrait: '… you would hardly believe how difficult it is to place a figure alone on a canvas, and to concentrate all the interest on this single and unique figure and still keep it living and real'. Since its inception almost three decades ago, the annual BP Portrait Award exhibition has been characterised by the original and varied methods, in terms of composition and technique, employed by artists who face this same struggle, whether their portrait represents a single figure, a couple or a group. A stipulation of the competition is that works should be based on a sitting or study from life, and it is this personal connection between artist and subject that goes a long way to ensuring that entries fulfil Manet's ambition for a portrait to be 'living and real'.

As the curator of nineteenth-century collections at the National Portrait Gallery, I am used to 'reading' historical portraits in order to discover more about the life of the individual portrayed. Clues to their profession, status or position within a social or cultural milieu at a time before living memory, can be found in a portrait's composition, in the sitter's clothes or the setting in which they are painted. As a judge of this year's competition, however, I was liberated from this historical detective work, for here we

Breech!
by Benjamin Sullivan, 2017
Oil on canvas, 820 × 400mm

are concerned only with new portraits. (Another condition of entry is that a portrait must have been completed after 1 January the previous year.) My fellow judges and I were therefore required to focus on each portrait's formal qualities, on technical excellence and on how effectively it evokes the presence of its subject.

During the first round, the judges viewed 2,667 works as digital images. All work was considered anonymously – the names of the artists, their nationality, gender and age were withheld from the judges. Titles of works, which are revealed upon request, often provide clues to the identity of a sitter and sometimes their relationship to the artist ('my mother', for example). It took two days for my eyes to recover from paying such close attention to thousands of digital captures of portraits on a big screen. Faces, bodies, people, in quick succession – the images burning themselves onto the judges' retinas: 'No, no, no, yes! … Can we see a detail of that one please? What is the scale?'

The judges then viewed an edited selection of works 'in the flesh' in a nineteenth-century warehouse in east London. The room was crowded with portraits jostling for attention – some of the personalities represented were bolder and seemed to speak louder, while the quiet works waited patiently before receiving the notice

Every year, the exhibition features fifty or so utterly unique subjects from all walks of life, celebrating individual identity and rejoicing in the shared humanity on display.

they, too, deserve. We attempted to decode those portraits that appear to feature symbolic meaning and, while my own choices were frequently challenged, my mind was often changed by the point of view of my fellow judges. As the selection was whittled down, the works were laid out on easels in a random display, where their merits could be better judged in relation to each other. In the final stages, individual judges championed their favourite works, arguing for paintings on technical grounds and for reasons of emotional resonance and originality. Sometimes there was no argument – some paintings were just too good to drop.

When the annual exhibition is shown at the National Portrait Gallery, I always look out for ways in which works in the exhibition resonate with works in the permanent collection – a playful re-working of a composition, perhaps, or a borrowed pose. However, for many visitors, the exhibition, brimming with brand-new paintings submitted from all over the globe, may, at first glance, seem quite unconnected to the displays of historic portraits on the upper floors of the Gallery. Founded in 1856 to collect and display portraits of the greatest figures in British history, it sought to represent, in the words of Lord Stanhope (one of its founders, speaking to the House of Lords): 'those who are most honourably commemorated in British history as warriors or as statesmen, or in arts, in literature, or in science'. It was not merely a gallery of British history, it was meant to inspire visitors to emulate the achievements of the nation's greatest citizens. While the identity of the Collection has progressed considerably since Stanhope's time – to better reflect British society in terms of gender, race and class diversity, now and in the past – the Gallery's acquisitions and commissioning policies still prioritise the sitter's impact on British life.

By contrast, the annual BP Portrait Award is not tied to a national story or the status or achievement of those represented. Although some of the submitted and shortlisted portraits depict well-known individuals (and a small number of these have even been acquired for the Gallery's Collection), the competition is concerned entirely with what constitutes a successful painted portrait, regardless of the identity of the sitters. Every year, the exhibition features fifty or so utterly unique subjects from all walks of life, celebrating individual identity and rejoicing in the shared humanity on display. Over the years, many prizewinning works have been inspired by personal relationships and are documents of friendships, love affairs or domestic life. In 2017 the first prize was awarded to Benjamin Sullivan for *Breech!*, the extraordinarily tender portrait he made of his wife

nursing their baby daughter. Painted entirely from life, mother and child are shown in the artist's studio, with its bare floorboards and painting paraphernalia. Such highly personal images are not ordinarily associated with the National Portrait Gallery, which tends to display portraits that show the 'public face' of a celebrated figure.

I would like to suggest that in these very intimate and personal portraits of loved ones or close friends, fascinating parallels can be drawn between the exhibition and some of the Gallery's most popular and iconic works. The earliest portrait in the Gallery's Collection depicting friendship is also its earliest-known self-portrait. In 1554, the artist Gerlach Flicke depicted himself and the pirate Henry Strangwish in a diptych miniature, the pair having become friends as prisoners in the Tower of London. The portrait is clearly dated, fixing the moment of its making over four hundred years ago, but its story of shared experience and solidarity is timeless. Likewise, by virtue of the annual nature of the BP Portrait Award, the works in this year's exhibition will be forever tied to 2018. As a judge, I became fascinated by the idea of all these artists, working in eighty-eight countries during the preceding twelve months, making portraits. I imagined the artists choosing their subjects, the sittings, the hours of

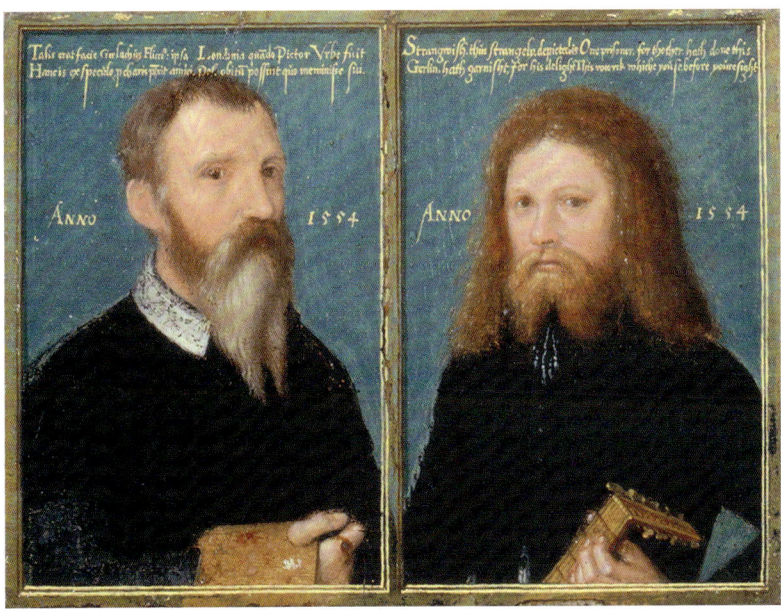

Gerlach Flicke (d.1558); Henry Strangwish (d.1562)
by Gerlach Flicke, 1554 (NPG 6353)
Diptych, oil on paper or vellum laid on panel, 88 × 119mm

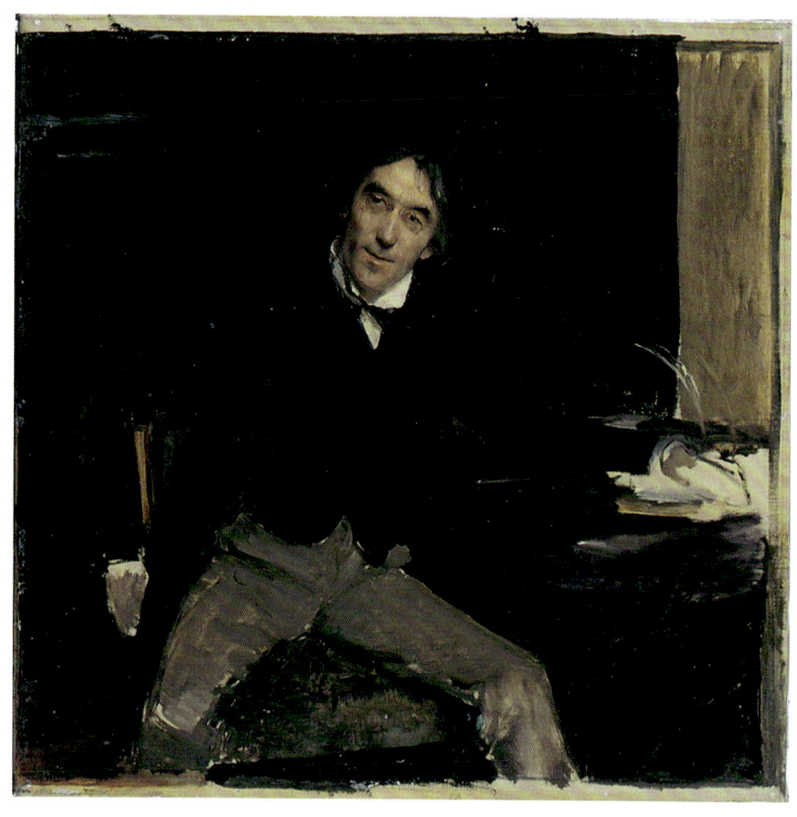

Sir Henry Irving (1838–1905)
by Jules Bastien-Lepage, 1880 (NPG 1560)
Oil on canvas, 460 × 475mm

work in a studio, and the moment when they decided to submit their work to the competition. Some artists, like Flicke, painted themselves – always the most reliable model and least likely to be offended by an unflattering representation. Others found willing models to pose – and in this year's exhibition these include mothers, siblings, brothers-in-law, friends, singular or in groups. Although the exhibition includes poignant images of illness and even of death, most of those depicted are walking about somewhere in the world, which is a novel prospect for a curator normally used to thinking about historic portraits whose sitters are long dead.

Finding a subject is only one of several challenges that artists may face, however. Some sitters may prefer their portrait not to be exhibited, let alone submitted for a high-profile competition such as the BP Portrait Award. When the French artist Jules Bastien-Lepage was visiting London in 1880, he asked his new friend, the great actor-manager Sir Henry Irving, to sit for a portrait, having become 'lost in admiration' of his face. Irving agreed, but came to dislike the result so much he almost destroyed it. In the work, he is shown at home in his study, and it is possible that the sitter objected to this informal portrayal as being too revealing of the man, rather than a portrait of the 'actor'. Irving wrote a

note about the portrait for his colleague and friend, the actress Dame Ellen Terry: 'I'm expecting Bastien-Lepage every moment. I'd cut up the nasty thing but think you like it.' Terry saved the work and eventually presented the portrait to the National Portrait Gallery – but only some years after Irving's death.

While many portraits in the Collection were commissioned for a public arena or intended specifically for the Gallery, others were never intended to be shown in such a venerated context. Branwell Brontë's group portrait of his literary sisters, painted around 1834, is one such work. When Charlotte, Emily and Anne Brontë agreed to pose, Branwell was just seventeen and had received limited artistic training. The work is unfinished and, as the pigment has faded, a ghostly self-portrait (painted out by Branwell) has revealed itself on the canvas. For decades, the portrait hung in the family parsonage in the Yorkshire village of Haworth, and was later folded and placed on top of a cupboard, forgotten. Consider how surprised Branwell would be to know that his teenage rendering of his sisters, re-discovered in 1914, now has pride of place, creases and all, in the Victorian Galleries – preserved for the nation as the only surviving group portrait from life of three of the most celebrated writers of the nineteenth century.

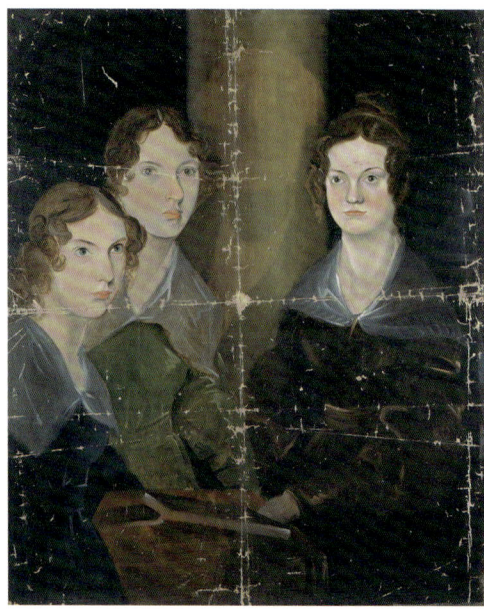

The Brontë Sisters:
Anne (1820–49)
Emily (1818–48)
Charlotte (1816–55)
by Patrick Branwell Brontë,
c.1834 (NPG 1725)
Oil on canvas, 902 × 746mm

The obvious shortcomings of Branwell's attempt to depict his sisters demonstrates that painting close friends and family can be just as challenging as painting a stranger. How is it possible for an artist to distil years of personal knowledge and the complexity of a relationship into a single image? Vanessa Bell's very small portrait of her sister, the great modernist writer Virginia Woolf, is one of the Gallery's most treasured works. Bell shows Woolf reclining in an armchair, crocheting – the sort of private moment witnessed only within the domestic circle – and makes no reference to her literary ambitions or, indeed, her progressive feminism. But Bell has chosen to blank out Woolf's eyes, her features appearing to dissolve in what may be an allusion to her intense interior life, but also to what Bell would not know or could not define about her sister. Woolf supported Bell's artistic career, and no doubt encouraged her radical approach. This type of support from a sitter can give a portrait painter the confidence and the opportunity to explore more challenging forms of representation – something that is evident in the BP Portrait Award competition, for which artists frequently make portraits free from the sort of constraints that are often imposed by a formal portrait commission, which tend to idealise or flatter.

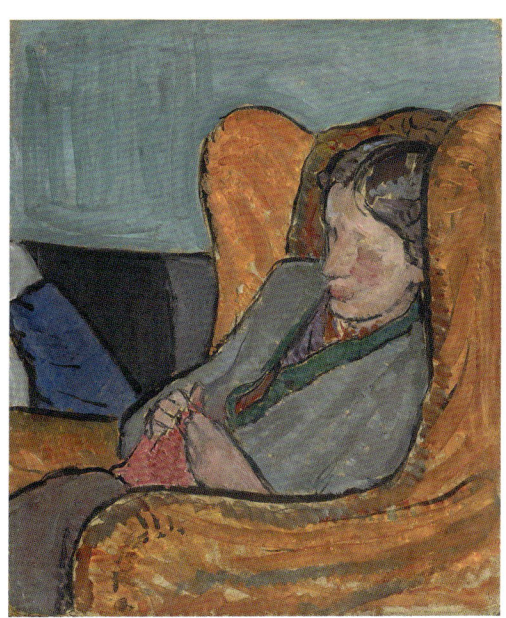

Virginia Woolf (1882–1941)
by Vanessa Bell, 1912 (NPG 5933)
Oil on board, 400 × 340mm

While some people sit with enthusiasm, others need a little persuasion. Of making his compelling portrait of a young Dylan Thomas, Augustus John recorded in his autobiography that: 'provided with a bottle of beer he sat very patiently'. John implies that the great poet was like a child, totally compliant if given his favourite treat – and this accords with the incredibly fresh-faced depiction in this portrait. Although still in his twenties, by the time this portrait was made, Thomas had already secured literary fame with two volumes of poetry, and had become a fixture of Bohemian circles in London's Soho and Fitzrovia, where he had met the famous bon-viveur Augustus John. John introduced Thomas to his future wife, Caitlin Macnamara, and this portrait was made shortly after their marriage. John's affection for his fellow Welshman is strongly felt in this work, which is comparable in its tenderness to the artist's portraits of his own children.

When considering thousands of entries for this year's BP Portrait Award competition, it quickly became clear just how much artists care about their sitters, just as Augustus John cared for Dylan Thomas, or Gerlach Flicke for his pirate friend Henry Strangwish. Artistic excellence aside, the works selected for this year's exhibition are

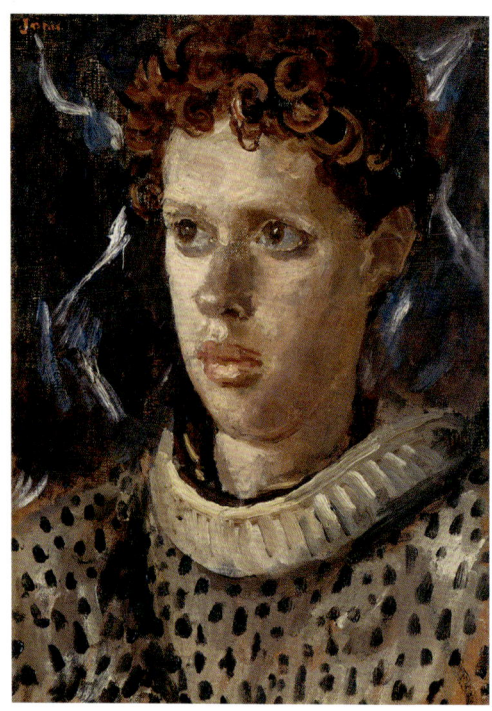

Dylan Thomas (1914–53)
by Augustus John, c.1937–8 (NPG L213)
Oil on canvas, 457 × 337mm

those that transmit to the viewer
most effectively a strong sense of
connection with their subject. As
Manet observed, painting a good
portrait is a struggle – indeed, the
process of making one can
sometimes put enormous strain on
the crucial relationship between
artist and sitter. The best, as these
examples from the National Portrait
Gallery show, can resonate across
centuries.

BP PORTRAIT AWARD 2018

The Portrait Award, in its 39th year at the National Portrait Gallery and its 29th year of sponsorship by BP, is an annual event aimed at encouraging young artists to focus on and develop the theme of portraiture in their work. The competition is open to everyone aged eighteen and over, in recognition of the outstanding and innovative work currently being produced by artists of all ages.

THE JUDGES

Chair: Nicholas Cullinan,
Director, National Portrait Gallery

Dr Caroline Bressey,
Cultural and Historical
Geographer,
University College London

Rosie Broadley,
Collections Curator,
National Portrait Gallery

Glenn Brown,
Artist

Rosie Millard,
Journalist and Broadcaster

Des Violaris,
Director, UK Arts & Culture, BP

THE PRIZES
The BP Portrait Awards are:

First Prize
£35,000, plus at the Gallery's discretion a commission valued at £7,000.
Miriam Escofet

Second Prize
£12,000
Felicia Forte

Third Prize
£10,000
Zhu Tongyao

BP Young Artist Award
£9,000
Ania Hobson

PRIZEWINNING
PORTRAITS

An Angel at my Table
Miriam Escofet

Oil on linen over panel
1000 × 700mm

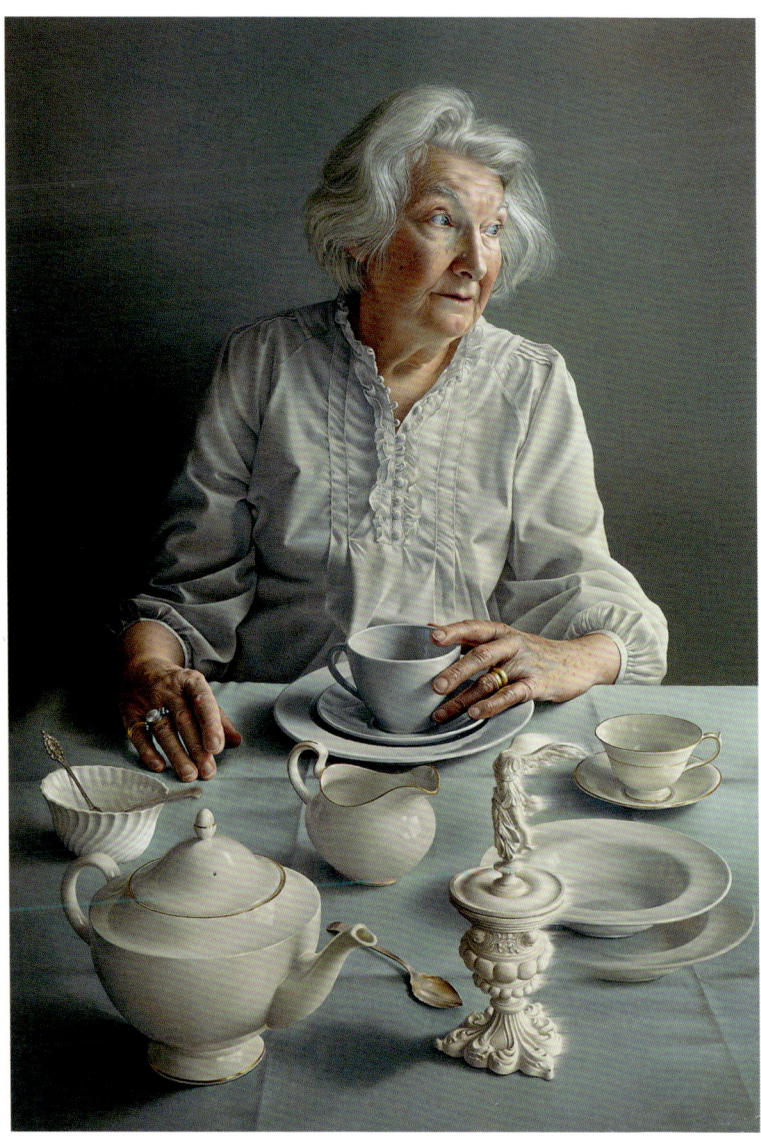

Miriam Escofet was born in Barcelona in 1967, the daughter of Spanish artist José Escofet whose work has had a lasting influence on his daughter's own creative imagination.

'Both my parents are artists and created a beautiful home full of artefacts, books and Spanish church statuary that they found over the years in antique markets,' recalls Escofet. 'These sacred items and the energy they emanated were hugely inspirational. They were my first experience of the power and magic of art and the magnetism of objects.'

In 1979, the family moved to the UK where Escofet graduated in 3D design and ceramics at Brighton College of Art. Self-taught in painting, she held her first solo exhibition at London's Albemarle Gallery in 2001, and her classically inspired works now encompass still life, allegory, imaginary composition and portraiture.

'Drawing and making are still at the core of my work – you could say that I construct my paintings very carefully – and there is a strong sense of design behind the work,' she says. 'I like to play with ideas of figuration, combining working from life and the observed world with imaginary or invented elements that communicate something beyond the visible, merging these within the same composition.'

Her winning entry in the 2018 Award portrays her English mother, pictured at her kitchen table. 'My mother has a wonderful inner stillness and calm and I really wanted to convey these qualities in the work,' says Escofet. 'I chose to depict her surrounded by crockery, as drinking tea is one of her greatest pleasures and it also provided a device for making her hands a central part of the painting.'

The painting took sixteen months to complete. First sittings and drawings helped to establish the composition and were followed by a detailed pastel study before Escofet began the painting in her studio, using photographic references and choosing to work in oils for their 'unmatched depth and plasticity'.

Several layers and glazes were applied during the painting process to add subtleness and depth to the image, while Escofet's biggest challenge was working with a reduced palette. 'I knew from the start that I wanted the painting to be fairly monochromatic and to be a play of light and whites, with the only note of colour coming from my mother's skin,' she says. 'Getting the placement of the objects just right also took time, as I did not want them to overpower the painting. It was a kind of choreography that evolved incrementally.

'Ultimately, I think the portrait manages to express what I set out to communicate – something very particular and personal about my mother, but at the same time to transmit an idea of the Universal Mother, who is at the centre of our psyche and emotional world.'

Interview by Richard McClure

Time Traveller, Matthew Napping
Felicia Forte

Oil on linen
1830 × 1830mm

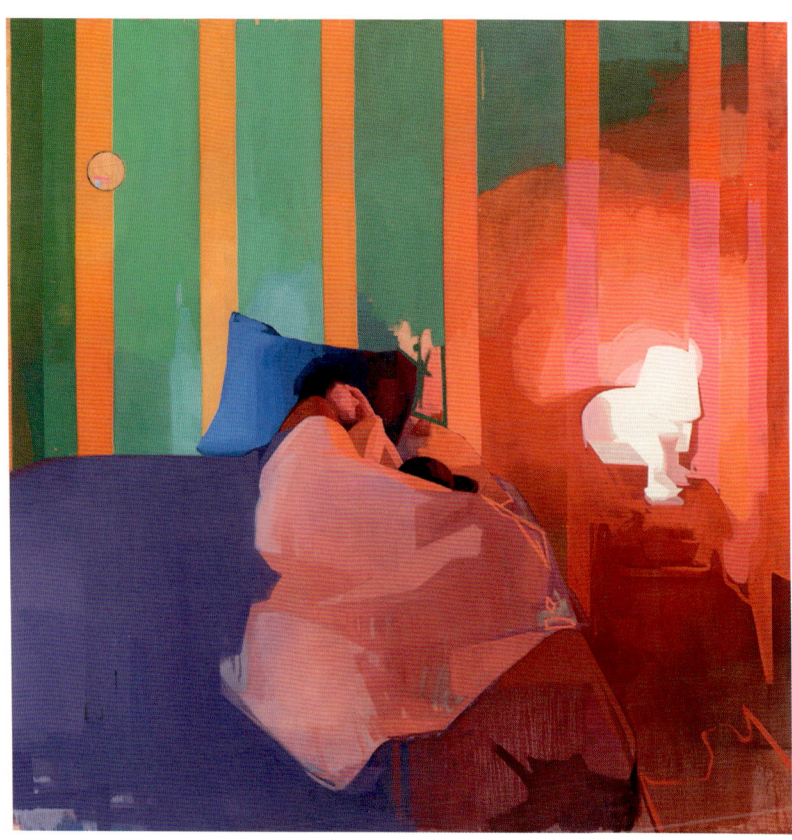

Born in Los Angeles in 1979, Felicia Forte describes her work as a visual journey, each painting a truthful record of her personal experiences – 'some pivotal, others simple' – and encompassing such subject matter as the contents of her refrigerator to the break-up of her marriage.

'Each painting I finish is a freeze-frame of my experience, understanding, skill and interests at the moment it was finished,' says Forte. 'Hopefully, if I'm painting something intuitively with integrity, then that will show up in the painting and other people will find some worth in it.'

Forte attended the Art Students League of New York in 2006, before moving to San Francisco where she worked as a waitress for several years before deciding to 'make a jump for it and see if I could fly'. Since 2010, she has been a full-time artist and painting teacher.

Forte lists her inspirations as the artists Euan Uglow and Félix Vallotton as well as the American illustrators J.C. Leyendecker and Dean Cornwell, for their 'craft, economy, innovative design and voice' – though her influences remain wide and varied: 'Currently I am in love with a takeout menu from a local fried chicken shop; it's so pleasingly designed I can't stop studying it.'

In 2017, she accepted a three-month residency at the Red Bull House of Art in Detroit, a project designed to attract artists to the city by offering accommodation and studio space. Her entry in the 2018 BP Portrait Award comes from her time there and depicts her boyfriend Matthew asleep in bed.

'I returned home one day and found Matt napping,' she recalls. 'It was a sweltering summer day, every fan in the house was on and every window open. It was a gift to observe this solitary and essential moment. I knew that I had to paint him.'

After stretching and priming a linen canvas, Forte worked in oils, placing two large rectangular palettes together for ample mixing space. She simplified only a few areas of the scene as she painted, including the wrinkles in the sheet and the amount of objects on the nightstand and floor. The colours in the completed portrait are almost identical to those in the original setting.

'A painting this size is an altogether different physical experience than painting a smaller portrait, and I had to practically dance in front of the canvas at times. I often jump right in to a painting without much preparation aside from the spark of interest and perhaps a compositional sketch – that's how this one happened.

'I wanted to remember Matt like that, relaxed but vulnerable, in the room he'd painted for me in vivid yellow and green, in the heat of the midsummer. I have preserved him. This portrait was painted of him, for me, and our lives will forever be cemented in my memory.'

Interview by Richard McClure

Simone
Zhu Tongyao

Oil on canvas
540 × 460mm

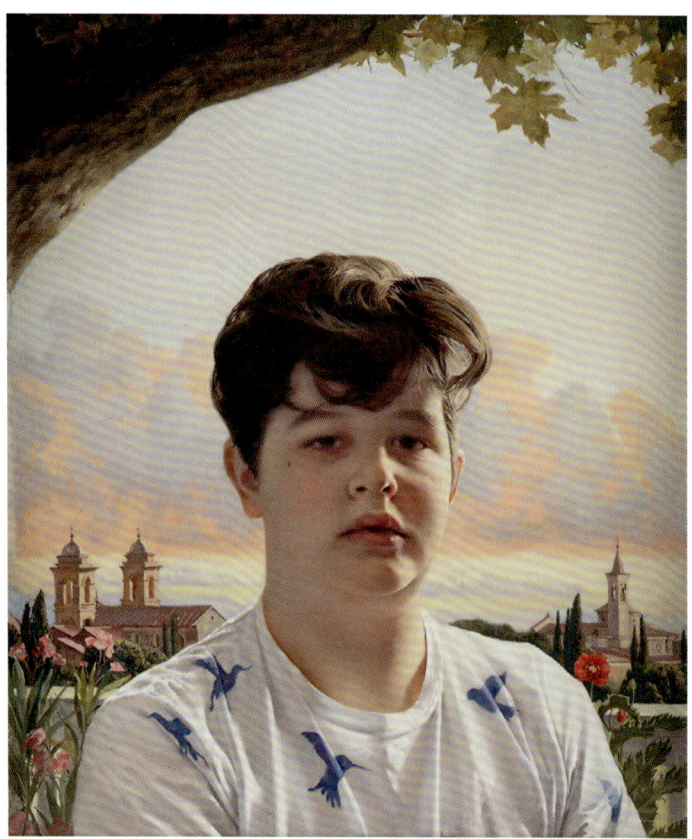

Chinese artist Zhu Tongyao was born in Jinan City, Shandong Province in 1988, and trained at the China Central Academy of Fine Arts. He currently lives and works in Beijing where he specialises in still life, nature studies and portraiture.

'I don't come from an artistic family, but my parents are enthusiastic art lovers, so this made an early impression on me,' he says. 'I always wanted to be an artist because art has been an inseparable part of my life. Every day's painting bestows value on my life and makes it meaningful.'

Among Zhu's influences are Sandro Botticelli and the nineteenth-century French artist William-Adolphe Bouguereau. 'I love Botticelli for his poetic expressions of vigour and vitality, while Bouguereau created a beautiful, idealised realm full of pure visual enjoyment, never hesitating to modify the reality in his paintings to pursue perfection. Both their expressions of nature and beauty are so vivid and incisive.'

Zhu has spent much of his working life in Italy. In 2015, he won the first prize for a work-on-paper at the International Biennial of Contemporary Art in Florence and the following year held his first solo exhibition at the city's Church of San Marco.

While in Italy, he was often visited by a local boy called Simone, the son of an Italian mother and an American father. 'Simone and his parents are kind and warm-hearted and they took care of me during my stay in Italy,' he recalls. 'Simone always came to see me when I was painting at home, so he became my model.

'One day, he came into my painting room, sitting near the window. The sunlight fell on his face and made me think of happy times spent with his family. I was deeply touched and wanted to create a portrait to express my feelings towards him and my thankfulness to his parents.'

The picture was completed in one week, with Zhu working on the canvas for five hours a day as he strived to deliver the 'inner nature and beauty' of his model. 'I do not have any fixed process since every model is so different from each other,' he says. 'If all my portraits used only one or two techniques they would feel numb and insensitive, as if made by machines. Paintings without soul.'

In this instance, Zhu started with preliminary sketches and watercolours in order to 'express my feelings at that moment, quickly' before painting the portrait in oils, his favoured 'means of expression'.

'In my opinion, portraits should always express the inner state of both the sitter and painter,' adds Zhu. 'The expression on the face is the most important part of a portrait. If the facial expression is not vivid, the painting loses its soul. In this painting, Simone has a positive expression on his face; I feel I managed to capture his sense of joy and peace in my painting.'

Interview by Richard McClure

A Portrait of Two Female Painters
Ania Hobson

Oil on canvas
1600 × 1200mm

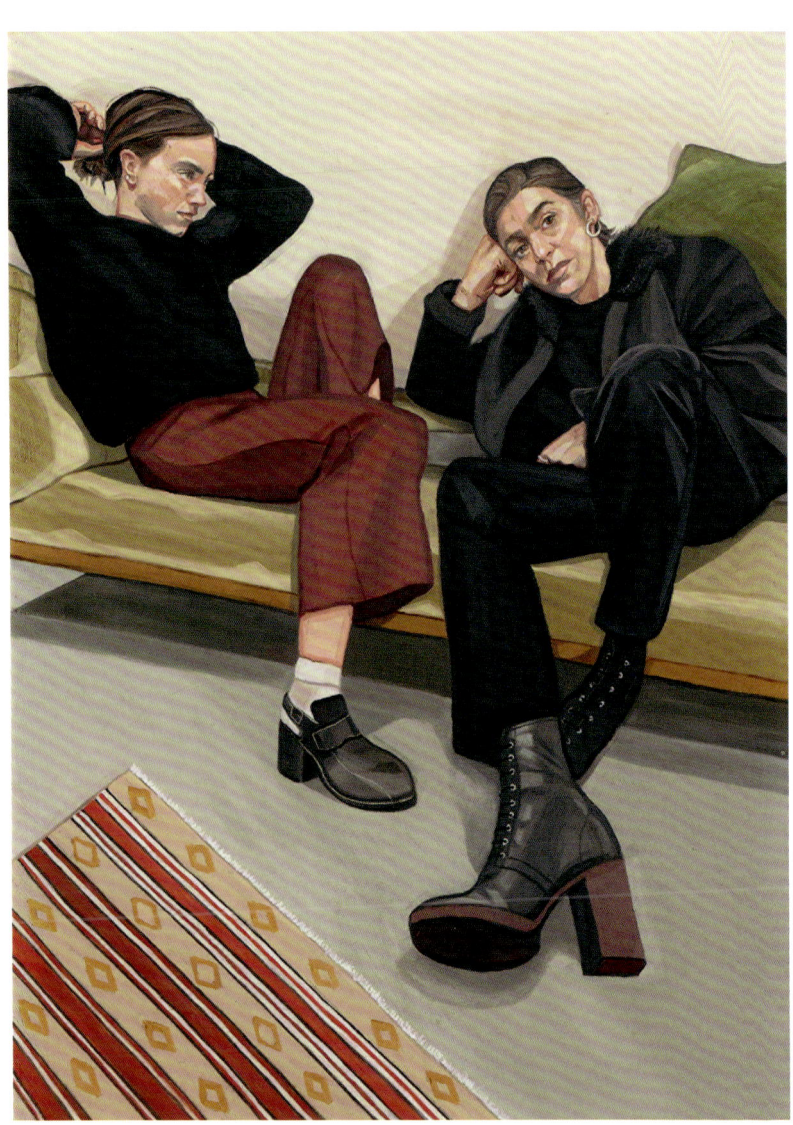

The winner of the BP Young Artist Award, Ania Hobson was born in 1990 and brought up on a smallholding in Suffolk where she started painting her family's livestock and local animals as a schoolchild. Hobson began selling her first wildlife paintings after graduating in fine art from the University of Suffolk in 2011, but has since shifted her focus to portraiture. Last year marked her debut in the BP Portrait Award with a self-portrait selected for exhibition.

'I started off painting wildlife because it helped me practise drawing from life,' she says. 'I still get a lot of sales from that side of my work, especially my fox paintings, but the growing interest in my portraits set in stone that it was going to be my main direction. For me, portrait painting is a way of preserving that person in that moment and time. It's a historical timeline that I think will continue forever.'

For her portraits, Hobson prefers to work on a large scale, allowing 'the paint to breathe'. After applying the initial sketch from life or photographs, she then works in oils and impasto, whereby the paint is laid on in thick layers so that the brush or painting-knife strokes are visible.

'I prefer painting fast as I find it more raw and in the moment,' she explains. 'If I overthink a portrait it can lose the passion. Impasto makes me focus less on the finer details and allows me to be more representational.'

Her winning entry in the BP Young Artist Award portrays the artist and her sister-in-law Stevie Dix, also a professional painter, who works at the same studio space in Suffolk. 'It's a place buzzing with amazing artists and I wanted to introduce a narrative about my relationship with Stevie as painters, and how it is to work in the studio together.'

Hobson identifies her use of perspective as a strong element in all her portraits, along with an interest in geometric shapes that introduce 'an abstract feel' to her figurative compositions. 'I use angles and perspective in order to create shapes which I then like to interlink with the interior,' she observes. 'This makes me look at the body more as an architectural subject. Painting the figures in black or dark colours emphasises the divide between the background and the subject. It's become my trademark.'

At a time when gender inequality is the subject of widespread debate, Hobson also wanted her entry to celebrate female artists and acknowledge those women painters who were historically denied recognition and exposure. 'In order to create a more powerful pose I changed the perspective into more of an upward angle, therefore allowing the boot to come forward and dominate the foreground,' she says. 'Art is not about just creating interesting pieces but also about building a story and this is an expression of confidence and strength.'

Interview by Richard McClure

**SELECTED
PORTRAITS**

Bruce Robinson, Writer and Director
Alastair Adams

Oil on board
920 × 750mm

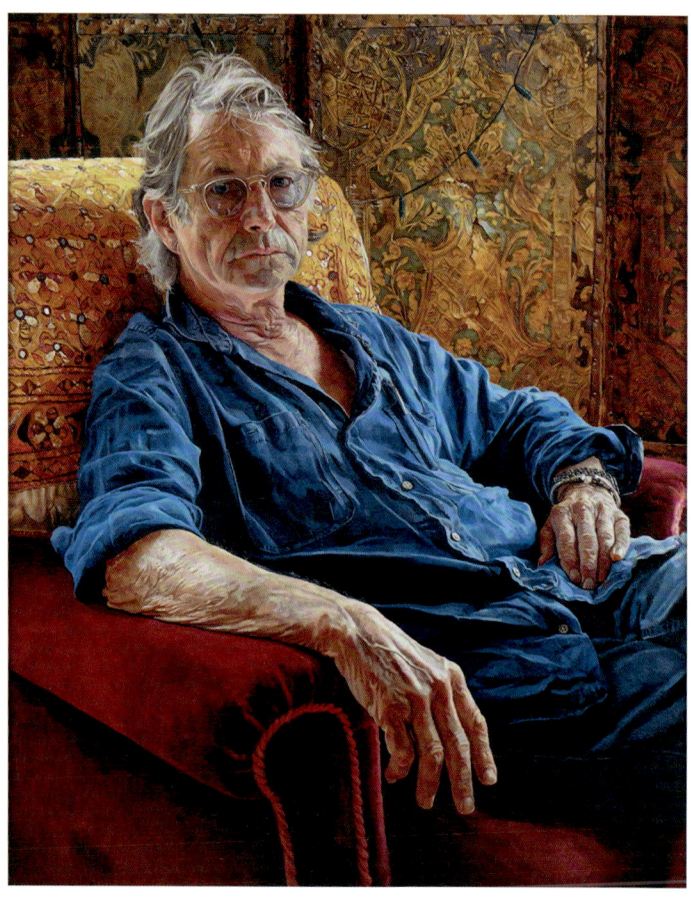

Girl with Long Hair
Annalisa Avancini

Oil on canvas
800 × 1000mm

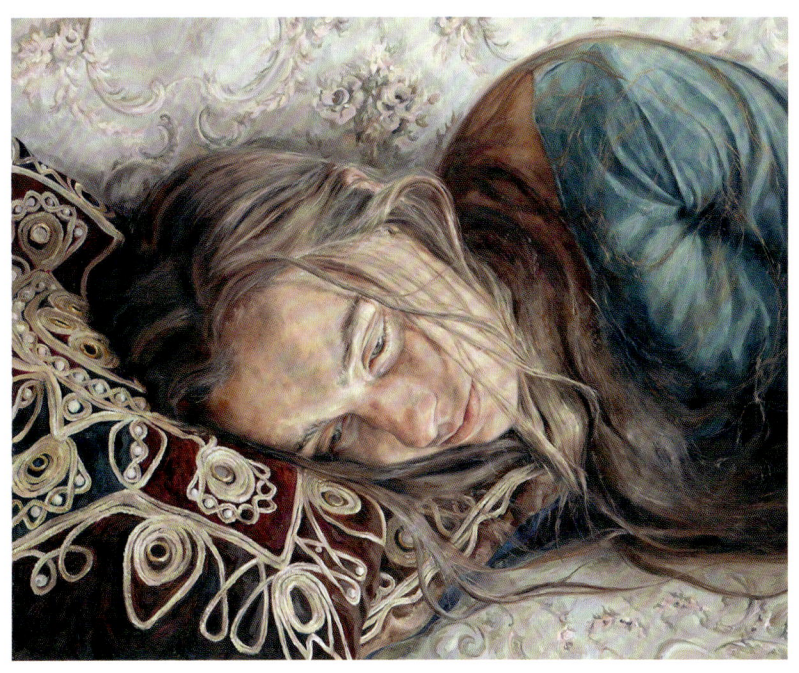

Tom Bedeman
Oliver Bedeman

Reverse oil on glass
940 × 640mm

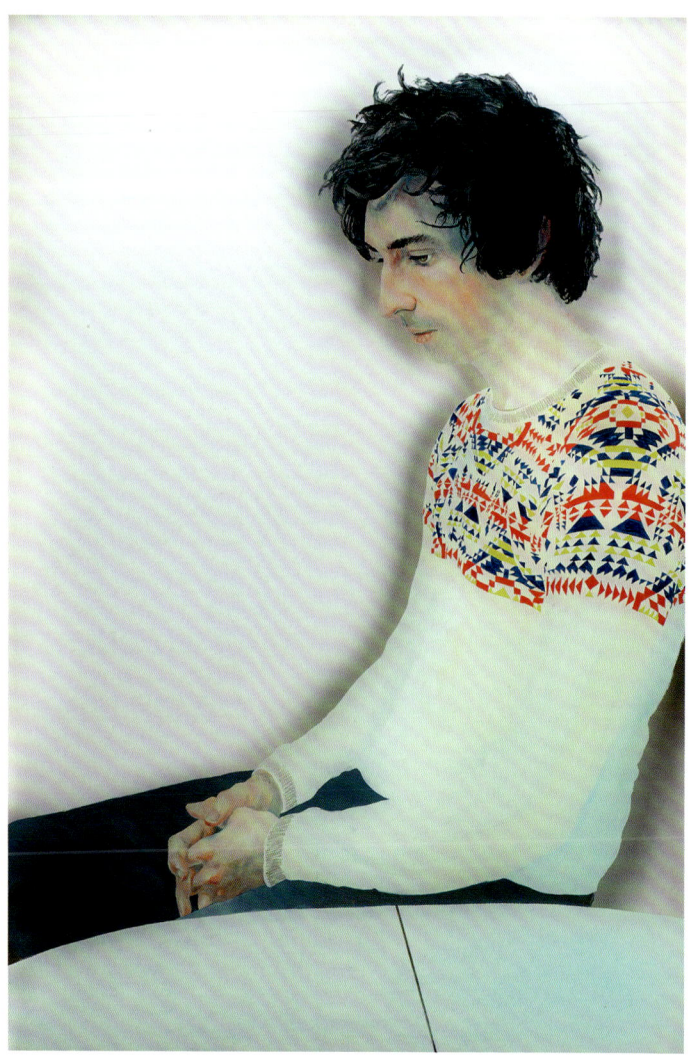

Transformations
Michael Bergt

Egg tempera and gold leaf on panel
280 × 230mm

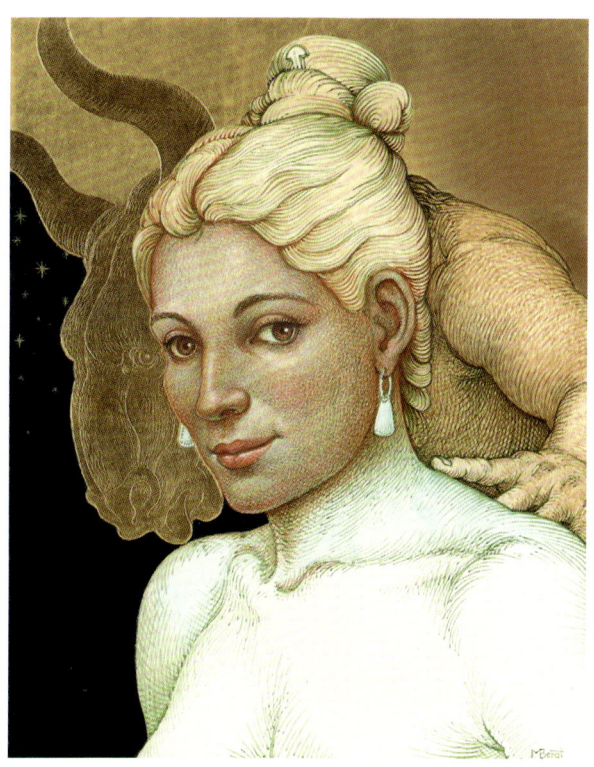

Portrait of a Girl (Becky)
Simon Thomas Braiden

Oil on panel
250 × 200mm

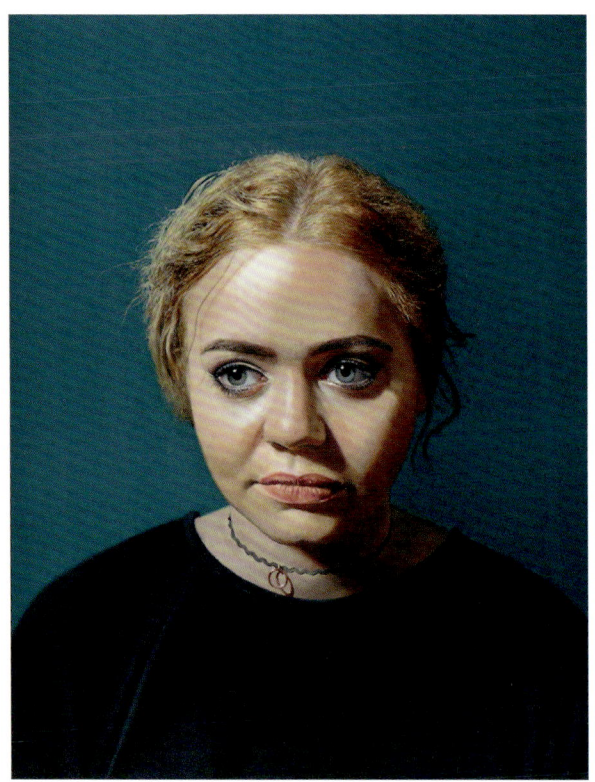

Fair Isle David
Shona Chew

Oil on linen
310 × 210mm

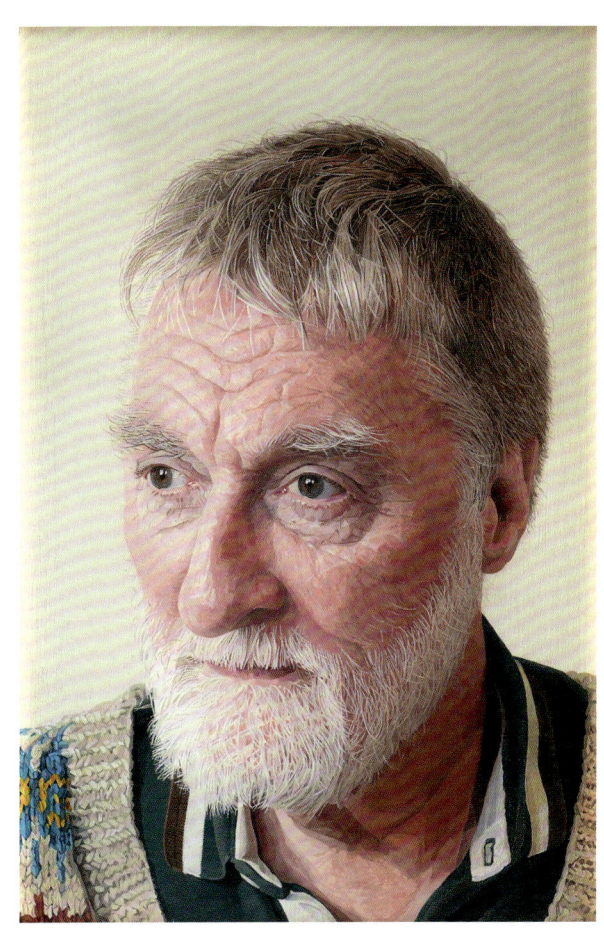

Broken Bodies
Jamie Coreth

Oil on linen
2200 × 1900mm

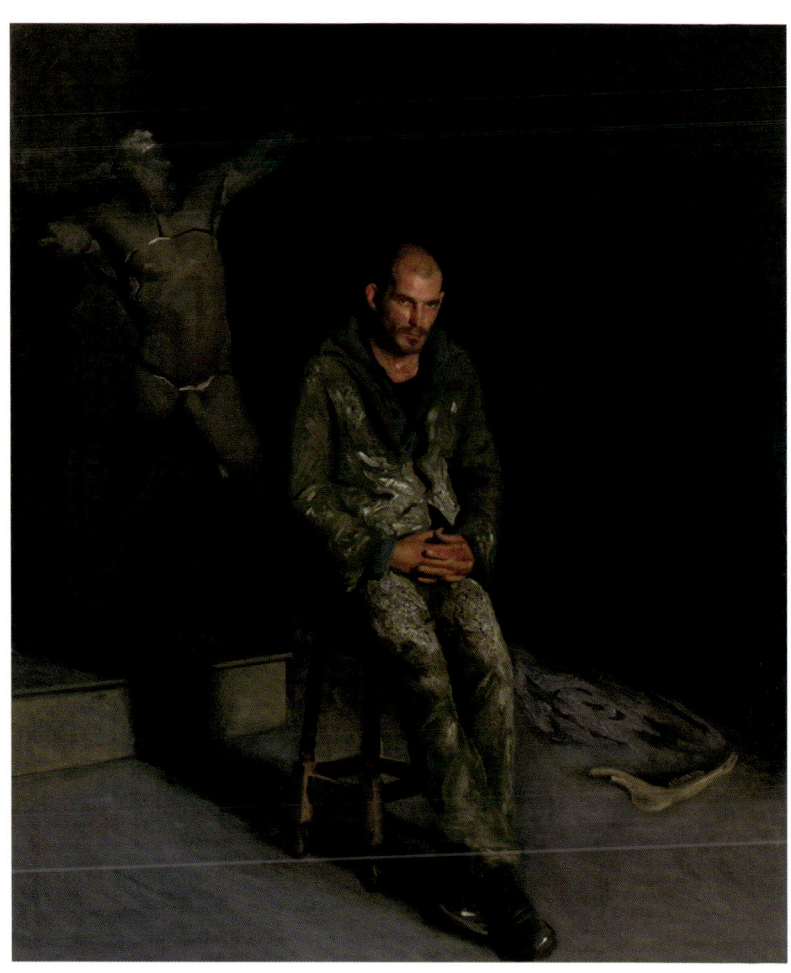

Miranda
Meghan Cox

Oil on muslin over panel
260 × 290mm

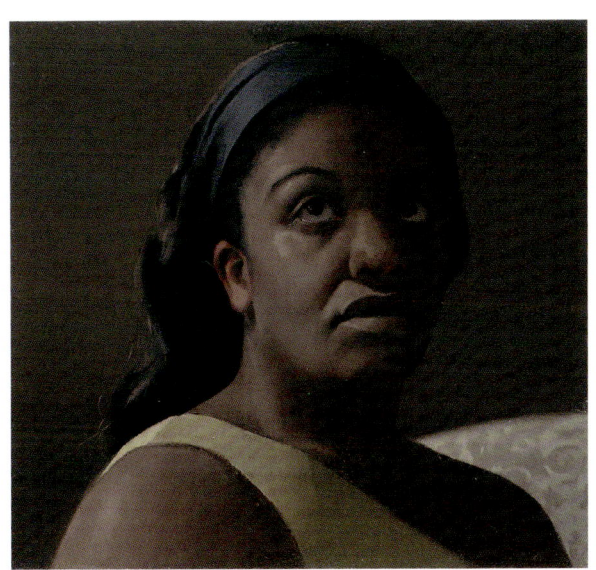

Quality Time
Éva Csányi-Hurskin

Oil on linen
760 × 1020mm

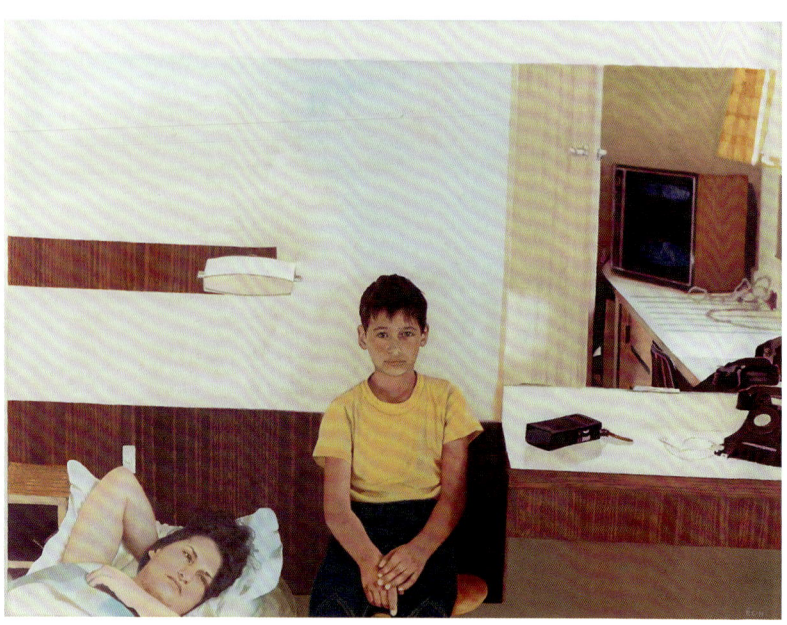

The Oolographer (in his study)
J.J. Delvine

Oil on panel
700 × 530mm

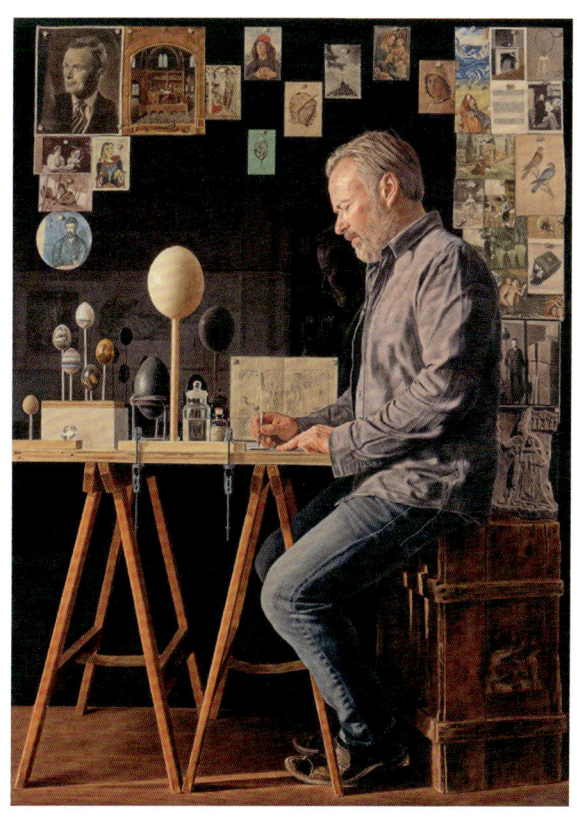

The Cholmondeley Children
Phoebe Dickinson

Oil on canvas
1500 × 1000mm

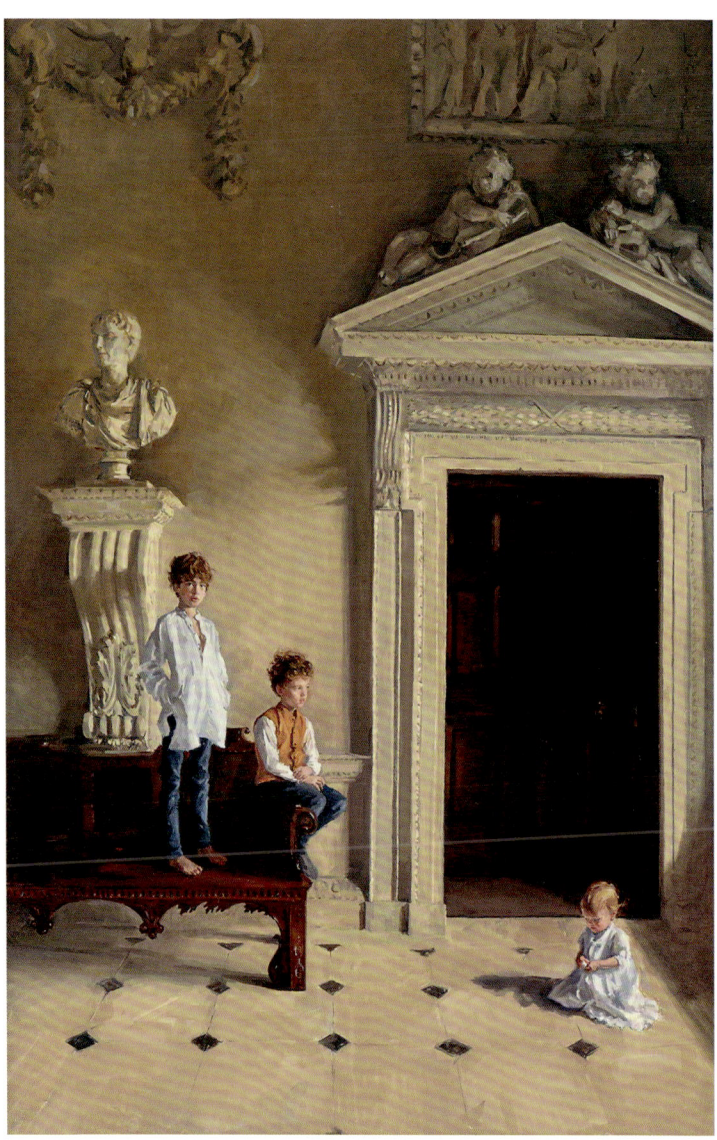

Claire Tomalin
Rebecca Driffield

Oil on linen
1500 × 500mm

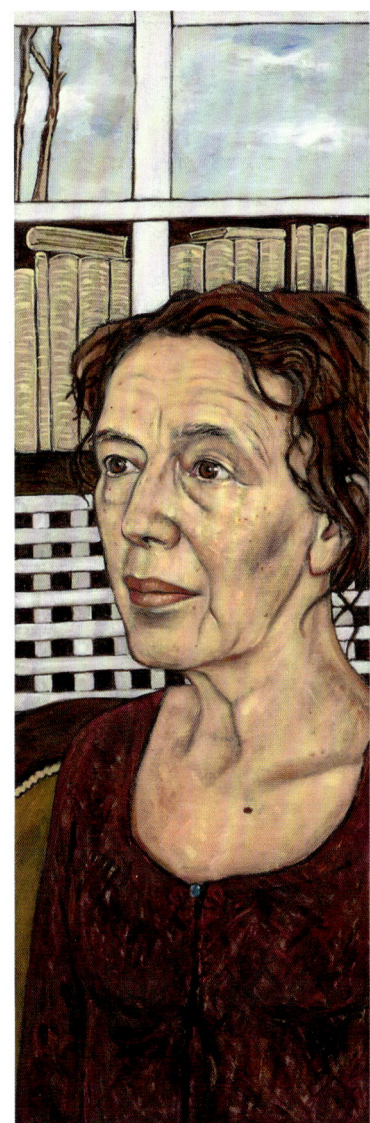

Portrait of Neema Tambo
Gaela Erwin

Oil on panel
1220 × 910mm

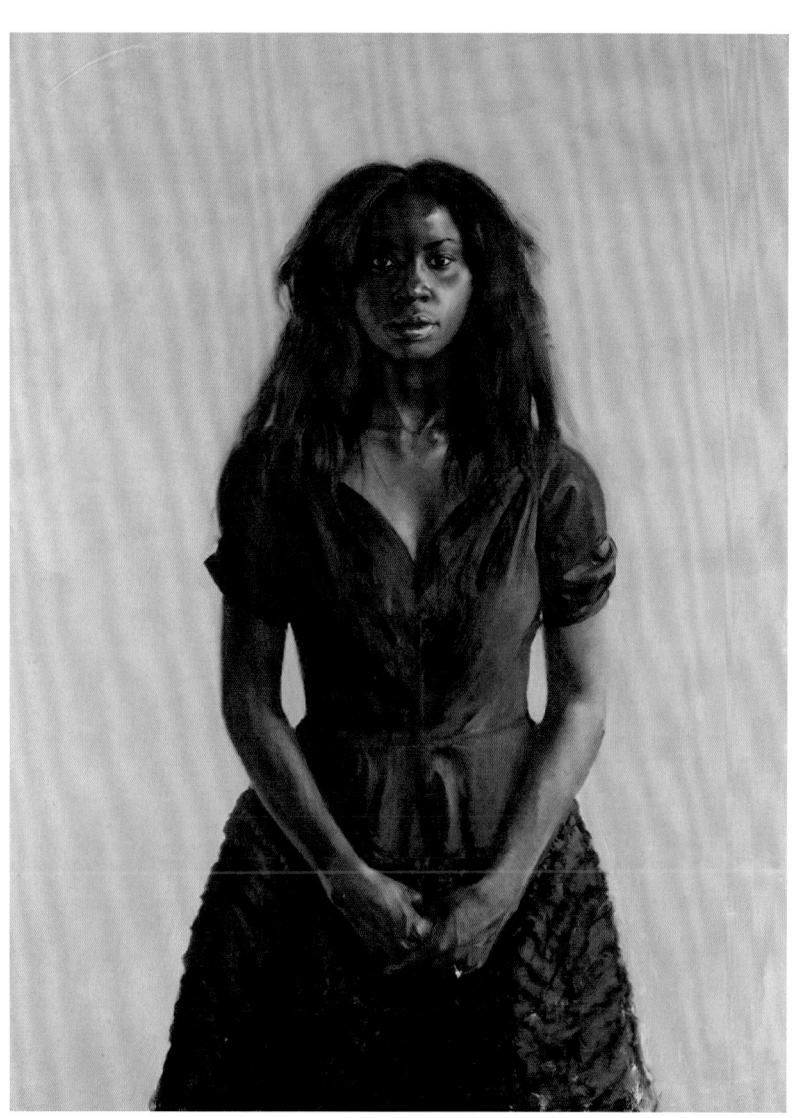

Found Albert Crouching in the Kitchen
Samantha Fellows

Oil on panel
400 × 400mm

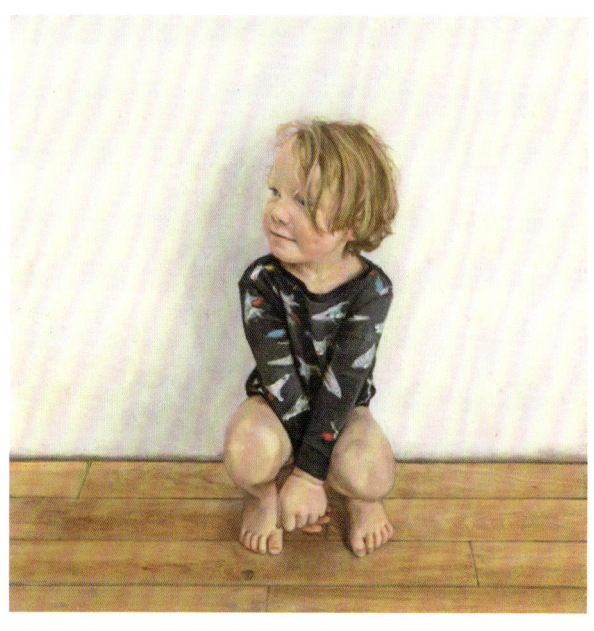

Tony Albert
Hugo Fergusson

Oil on canvas
1000 × 700mm

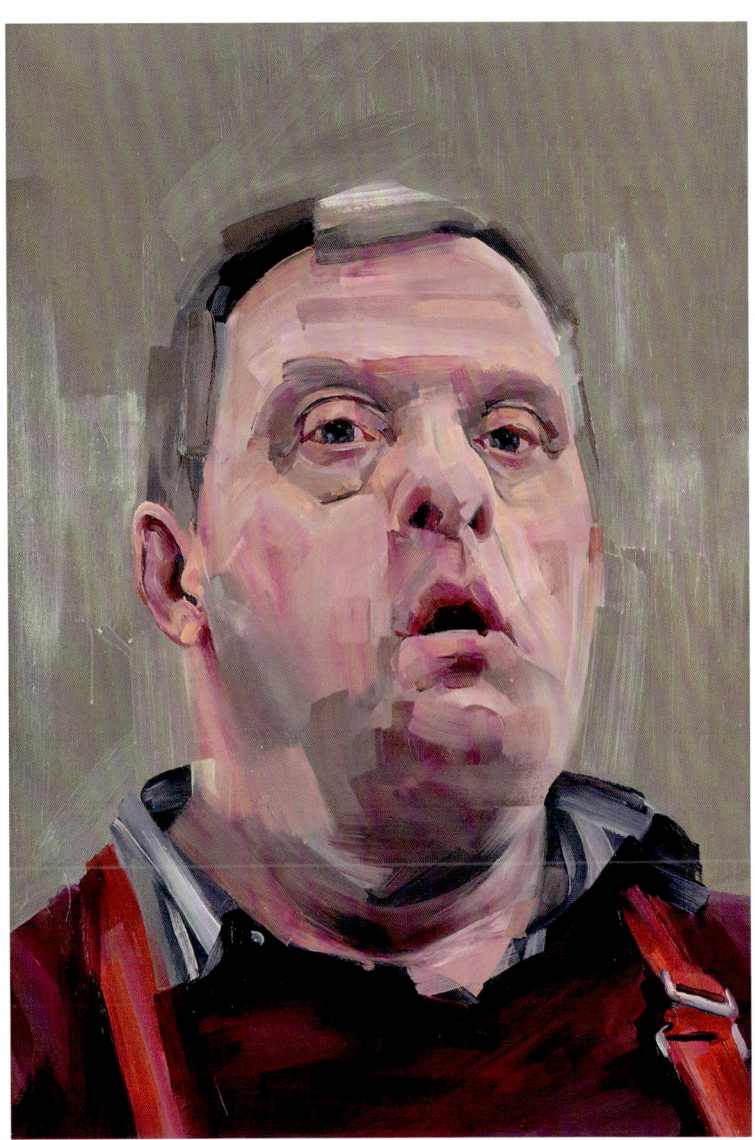

Robert
Peter James Field

Oil on panel
300 × 210mm

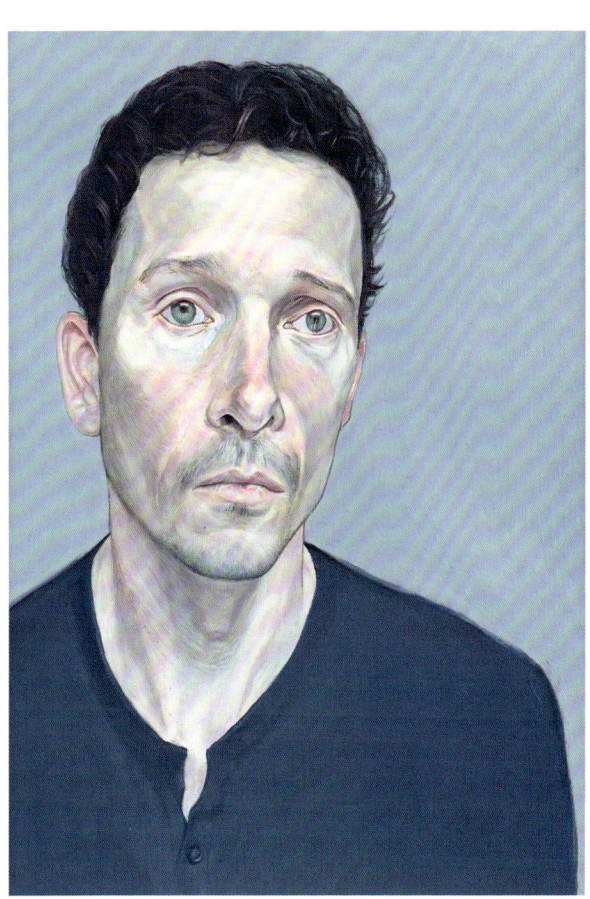

Dad's Last Day
Nathan Ford

Oil and pencil on canvas
200 × 280mm

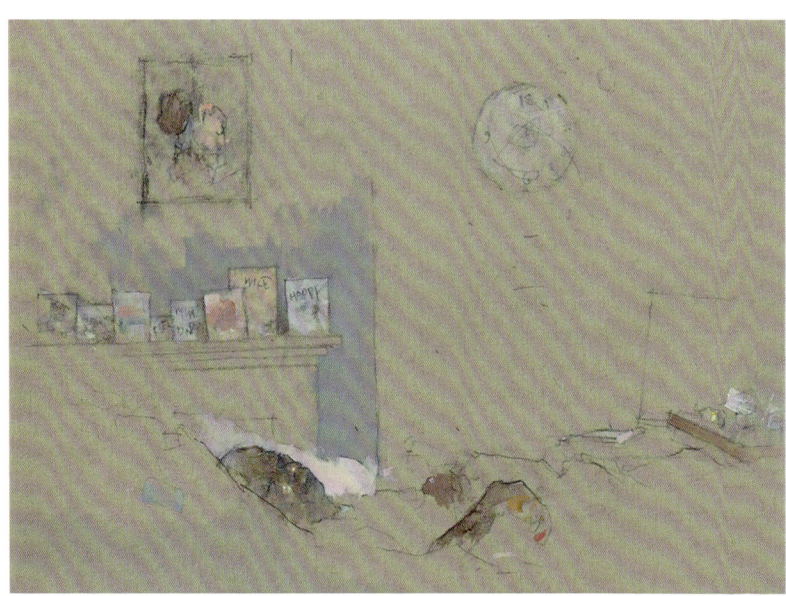

Tim and the Dog
Jack Freeman

Oil on canvas
490 × 360mm

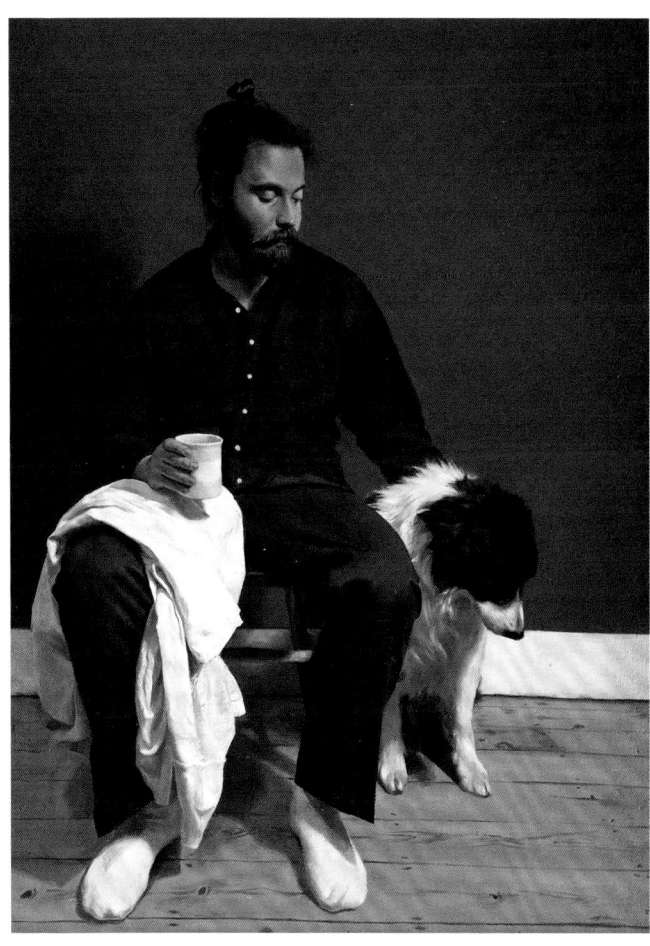

Francesca Hayward,
Principal Dancer at the Royal Ballet
Vanessa Garwood

Oil on canvas
1500 × 1200mm

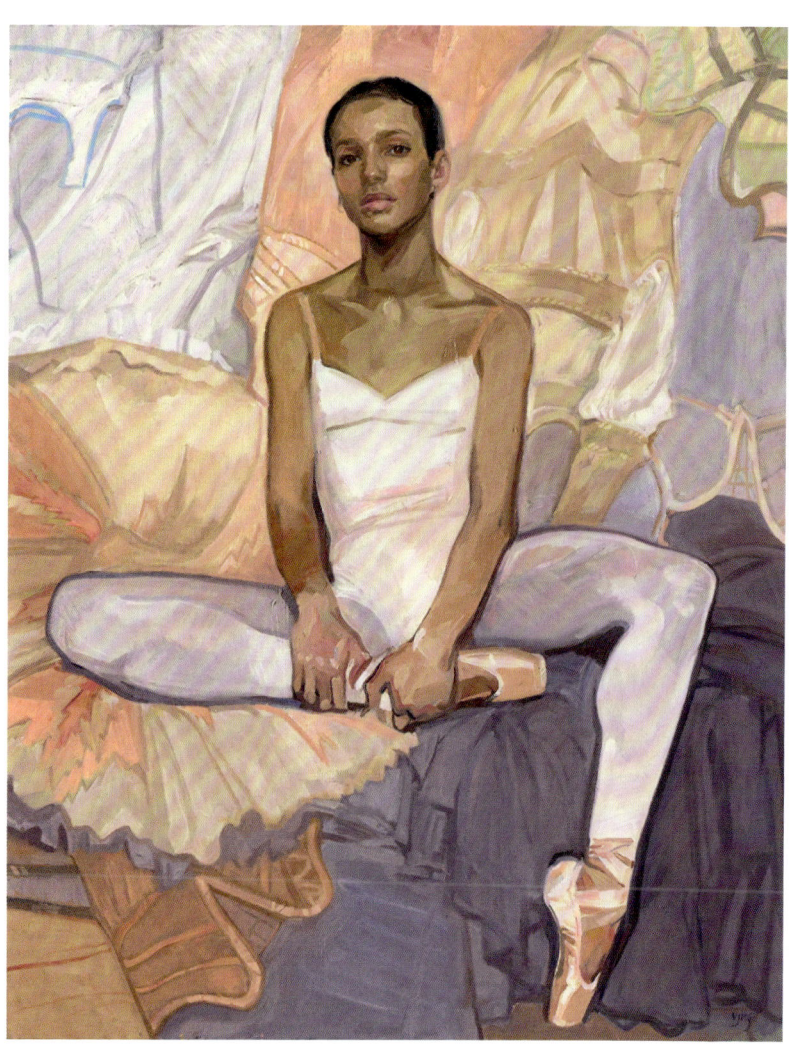

A Portrait of Gifty from Shitima
Huey Glynn-Jones

Oil on canvas
250 × 310mm

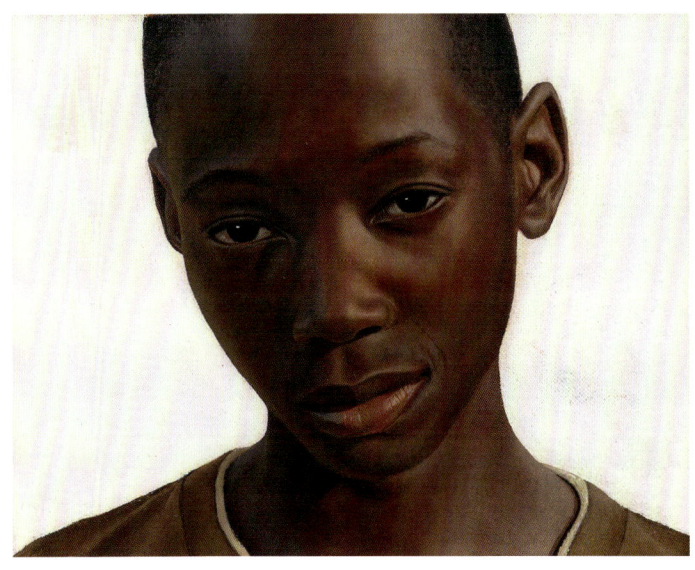

Self-Portrait
Seçil Güven

Oil on canvas
1800 × 1200mm

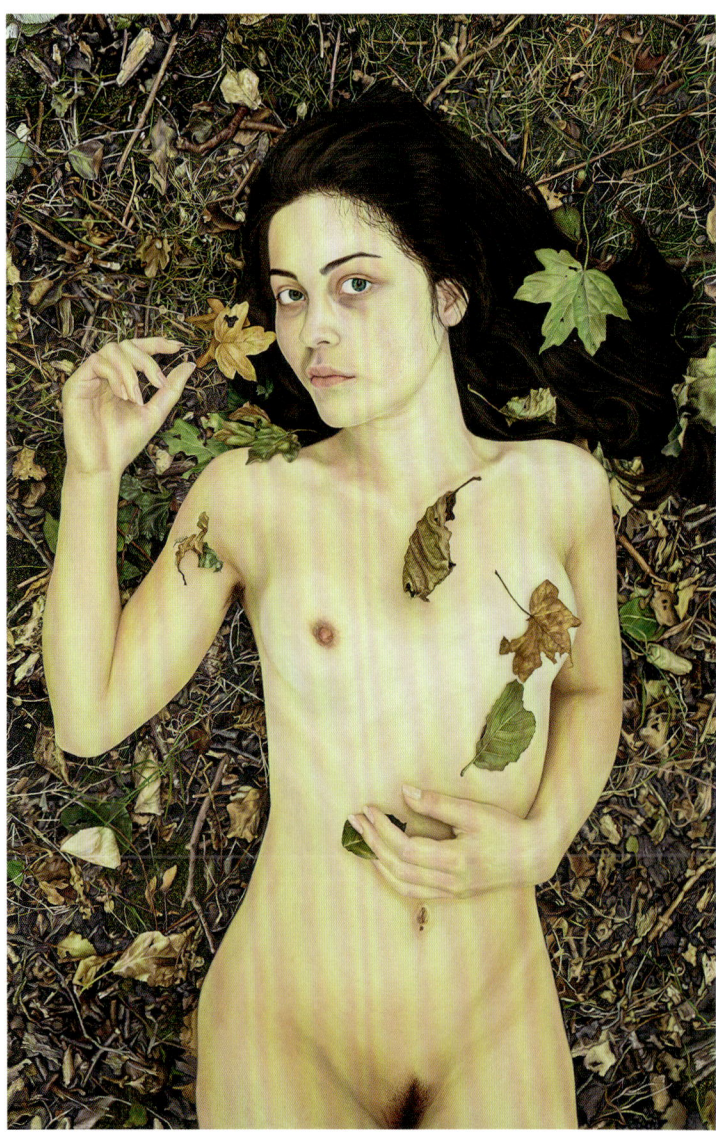

Ziqiang 124
Chunchieh Huang

Oil on linen
1460 × 970mm

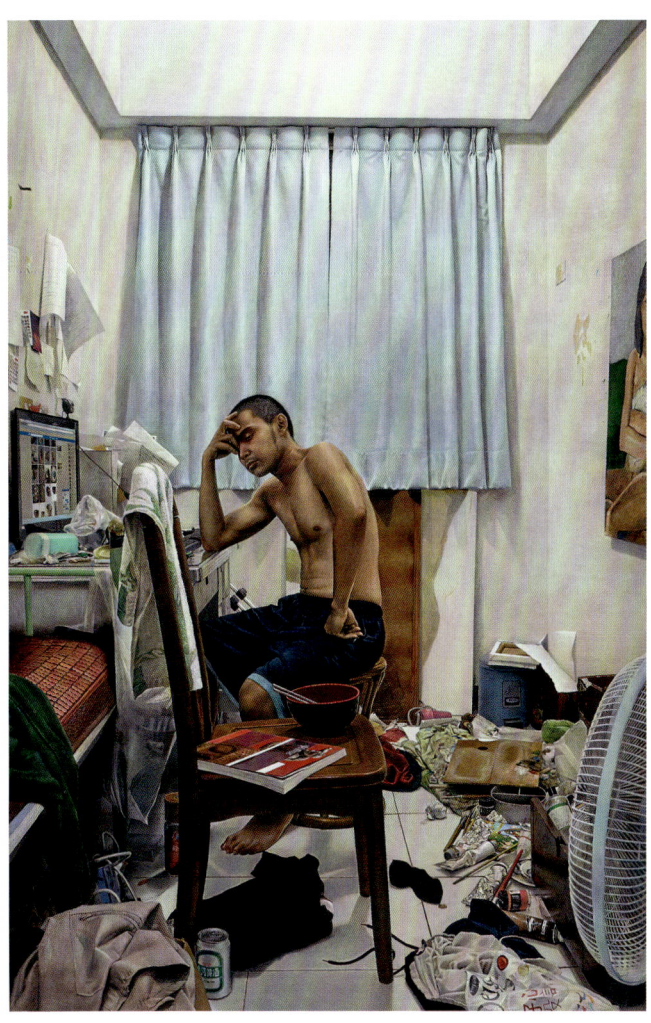

Mr & Mrs Cooper. Separated.
Mark H. Lawrence

Oil on canvas
700 × 900mm

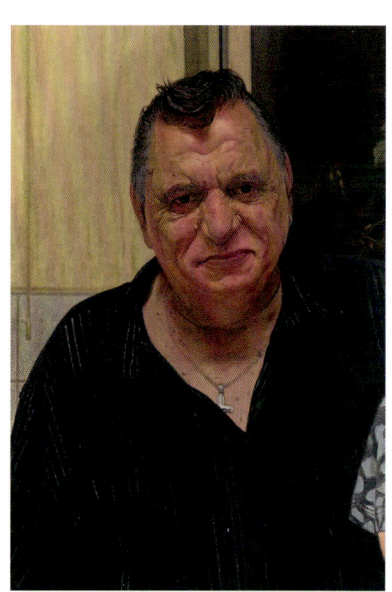 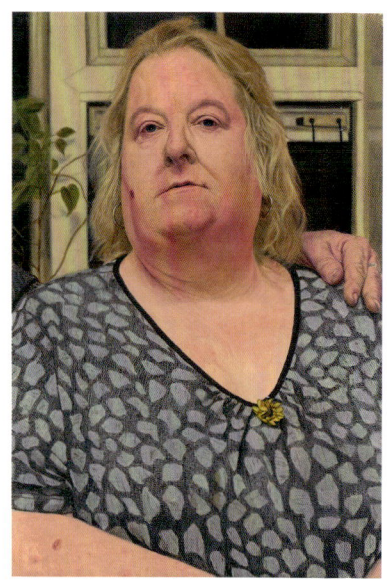

Verania
Antonio Lara Luque

Oil on canvas
1000 × 730mm

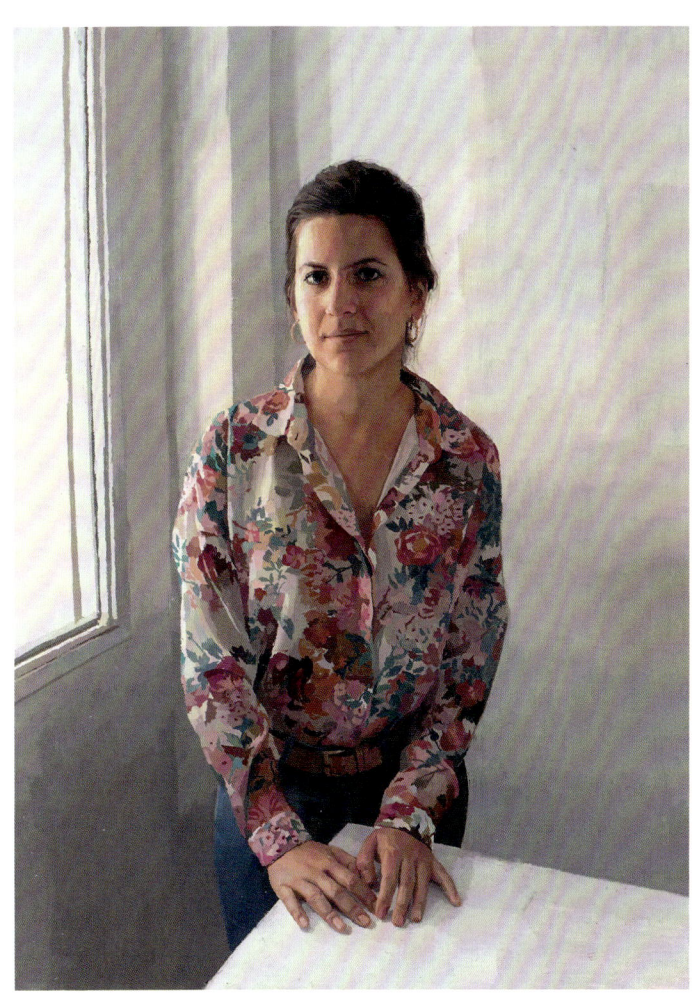

Derek (I Am)
John McCarthy

Acrylic on panel
700 × 700mm

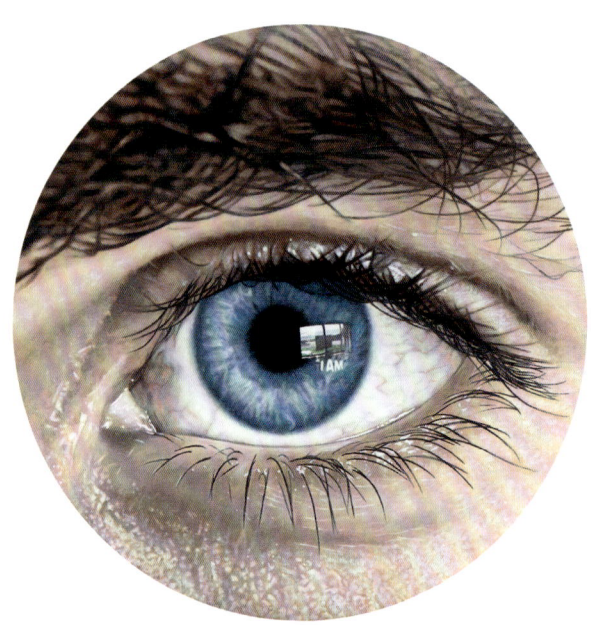

Laura
Shawn McGovern

Oil on board
790 × 520mm

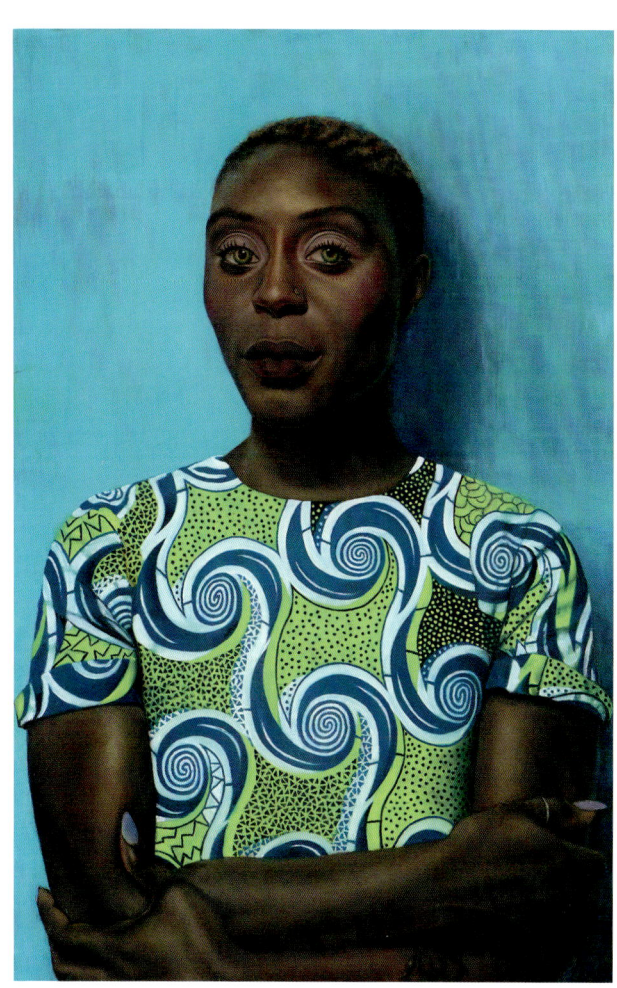

The Biologist
Miguel Ángel Moya

Oil on linen
1140 × 860mm

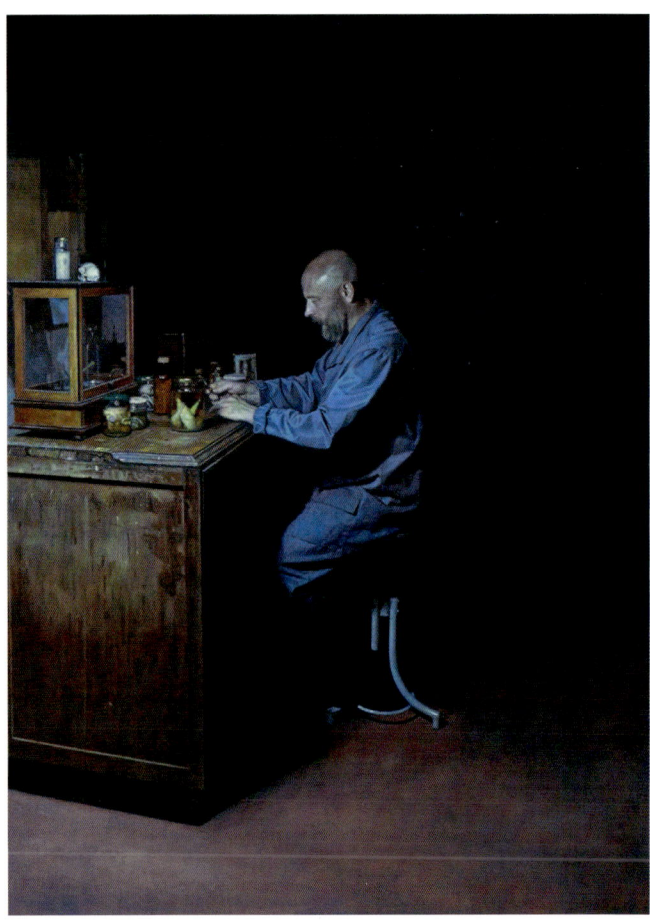

LTR Team A
Laura Nardo

Oil on canvas
1000 × 1000mm

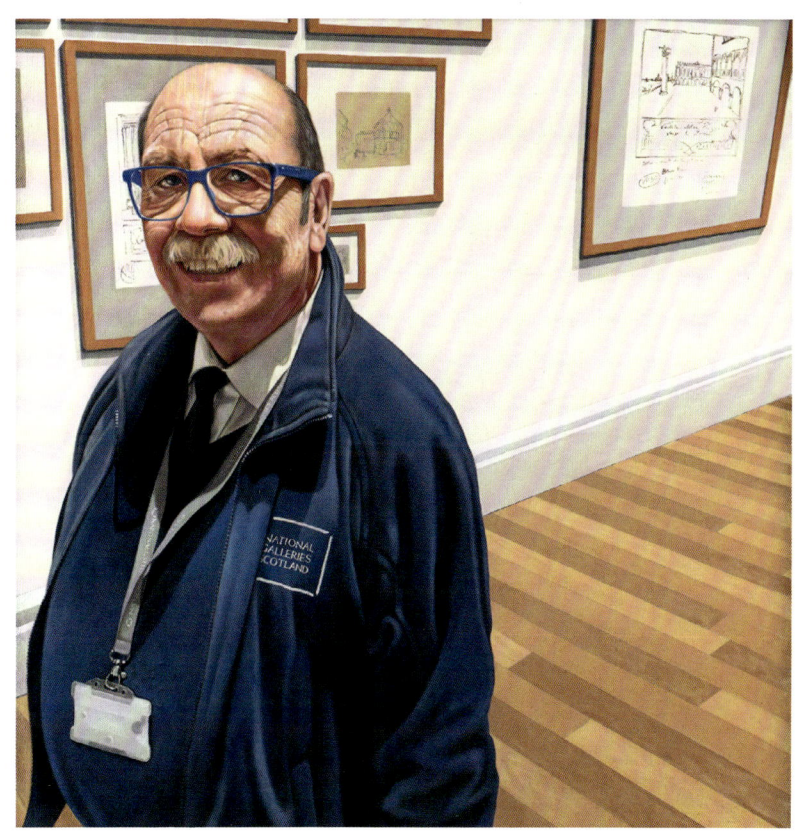

Charlie Masson
Alvin Ong

Oil on canvas
400 × 300mm

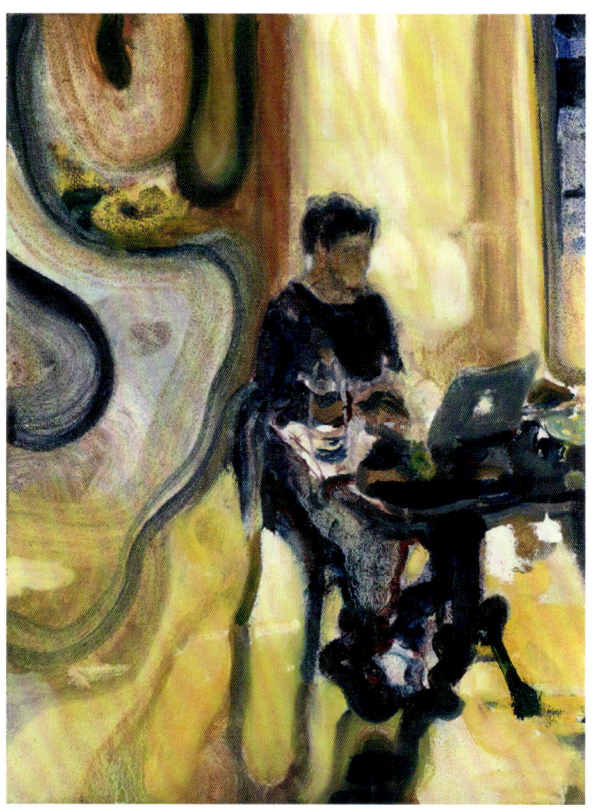

A Throne in the West
Massimiliano Pironti

Oil on panel
1000 × 600mm

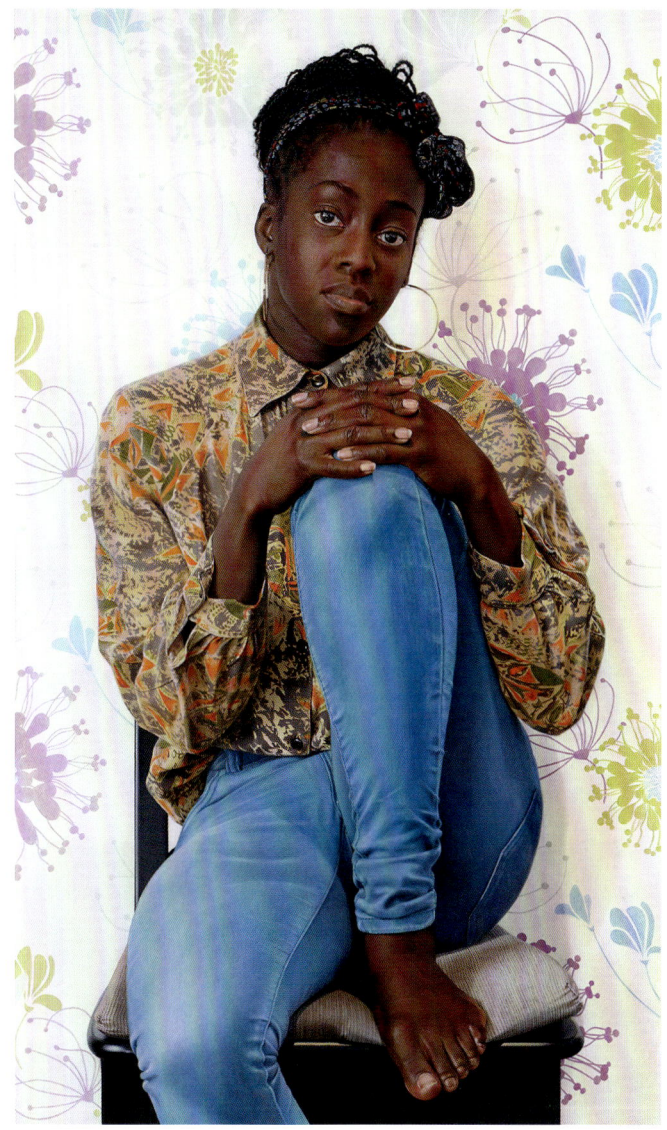

Mrs Anna Wójcik
Monika Polak

Oil on fabric
1000 × 800mm

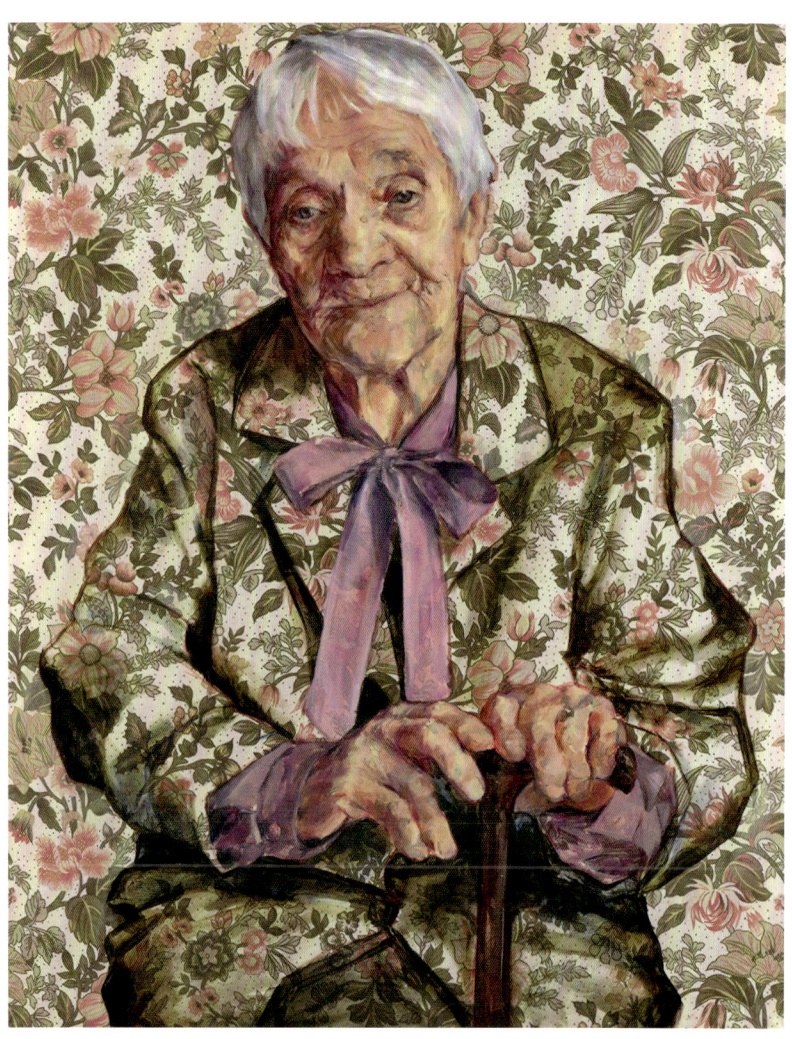

An Existential Crisis
Megan Roodenrys

Oil on linen
610 × 380mm

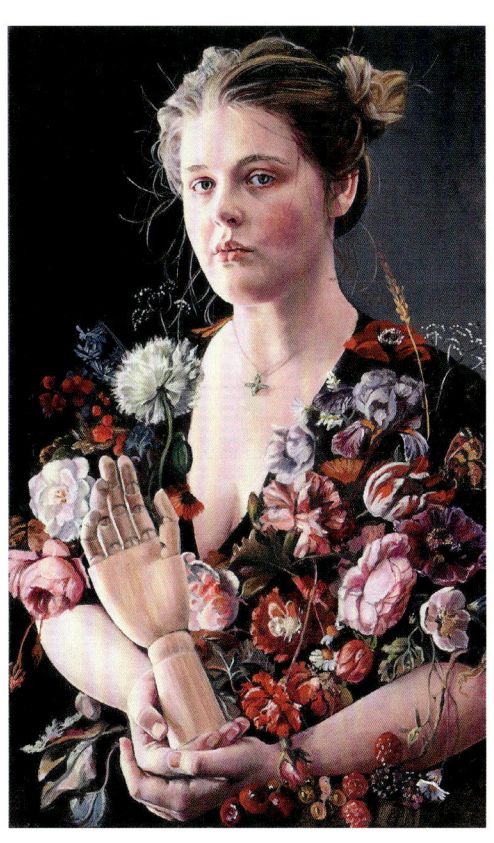

Ako
Nikita Sacha

Oil on panel
250 × 250mm

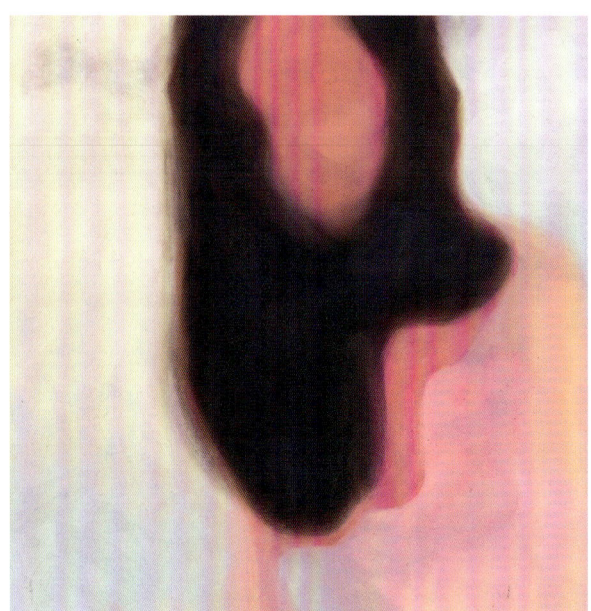

Bertha
Jesús María Sáez de Vicuña Ochoa

Oil on canvas
1500 × 1000mm

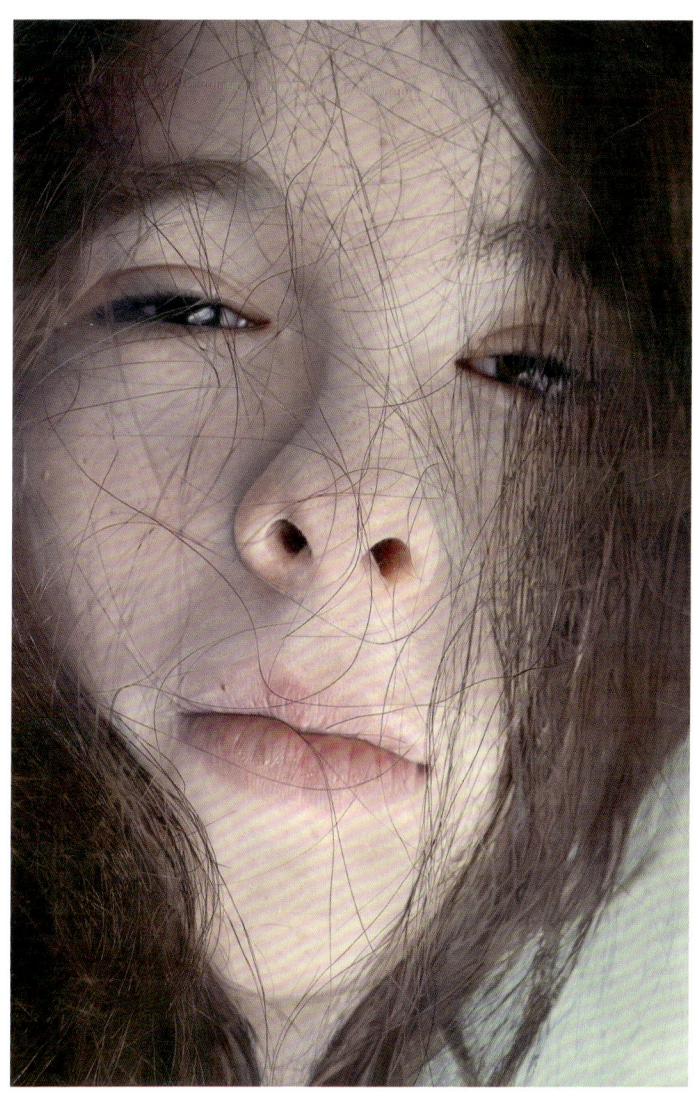

David
Robert Seidel

Egg tempera on canvas
440 × 310mm

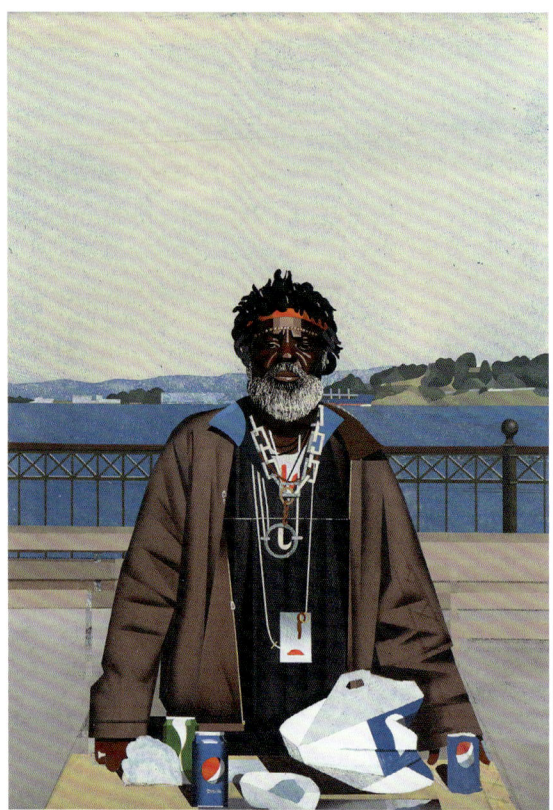

Vincent Desiderio
Bernardo Siciliano

Oil on canvas
1440 × 1090mm

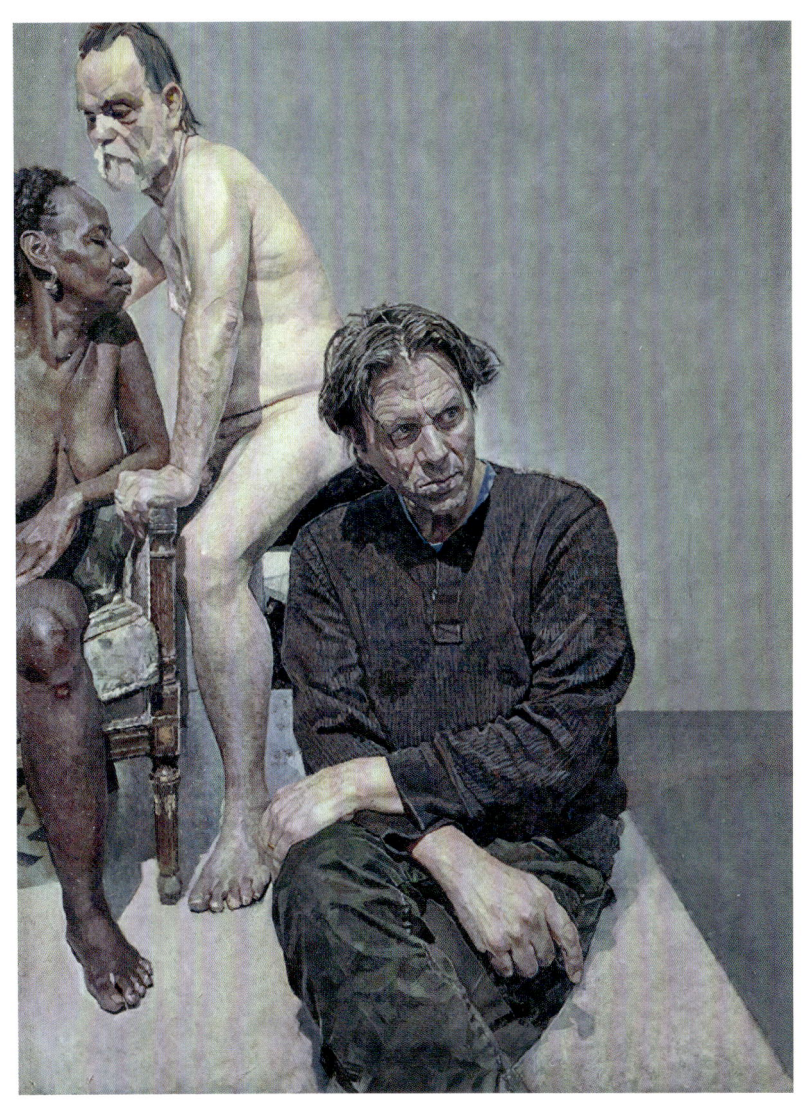

Self-Portrait
Liesel Thomas

Oil on panel
400 × 300mm

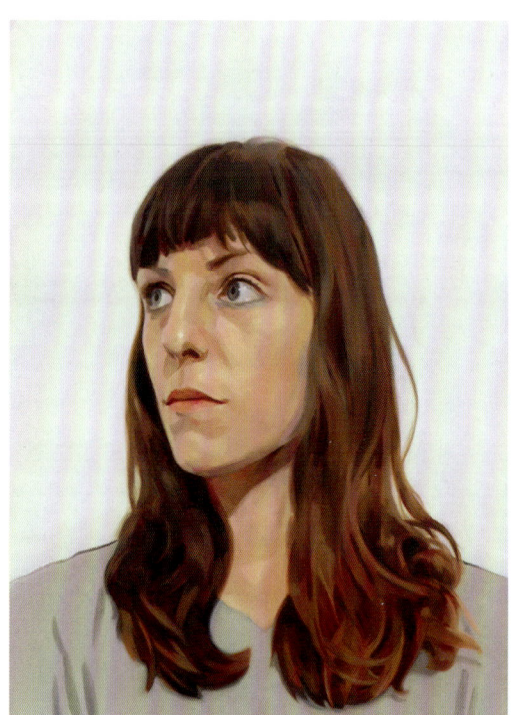

Finn
René Tweehuysen

Oil and tempera on linen
500 × 500mm

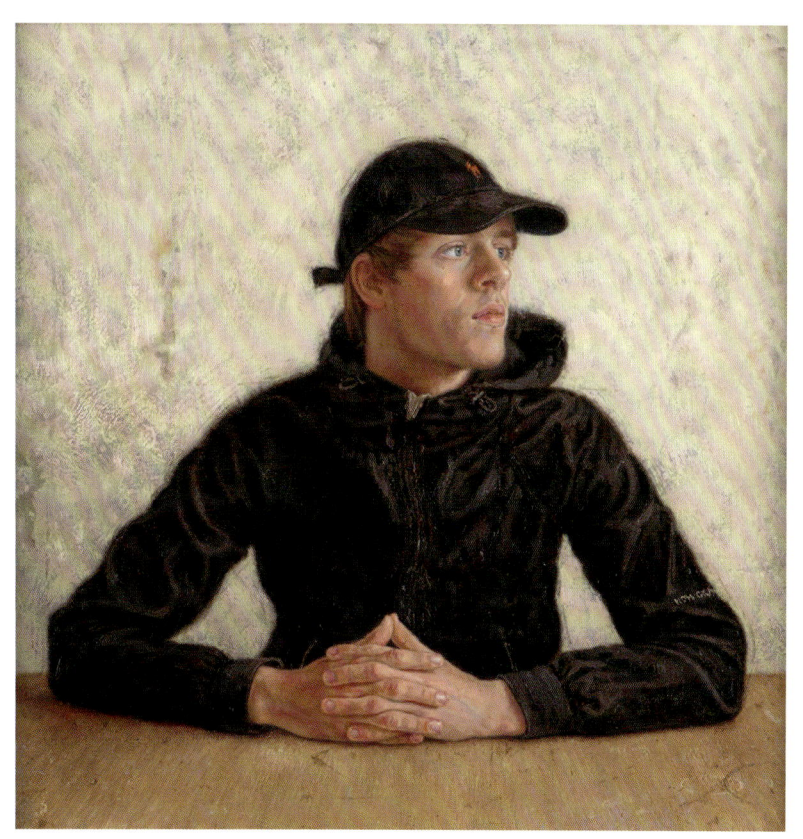

At the End of the Staircase
Fermín G. Villaescusa

Oil on linen
890 × 1160mm

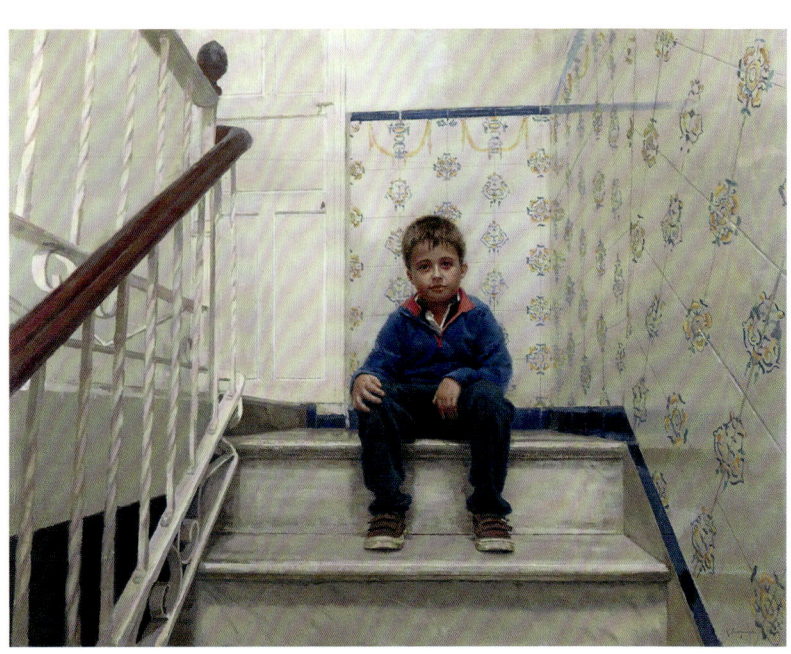

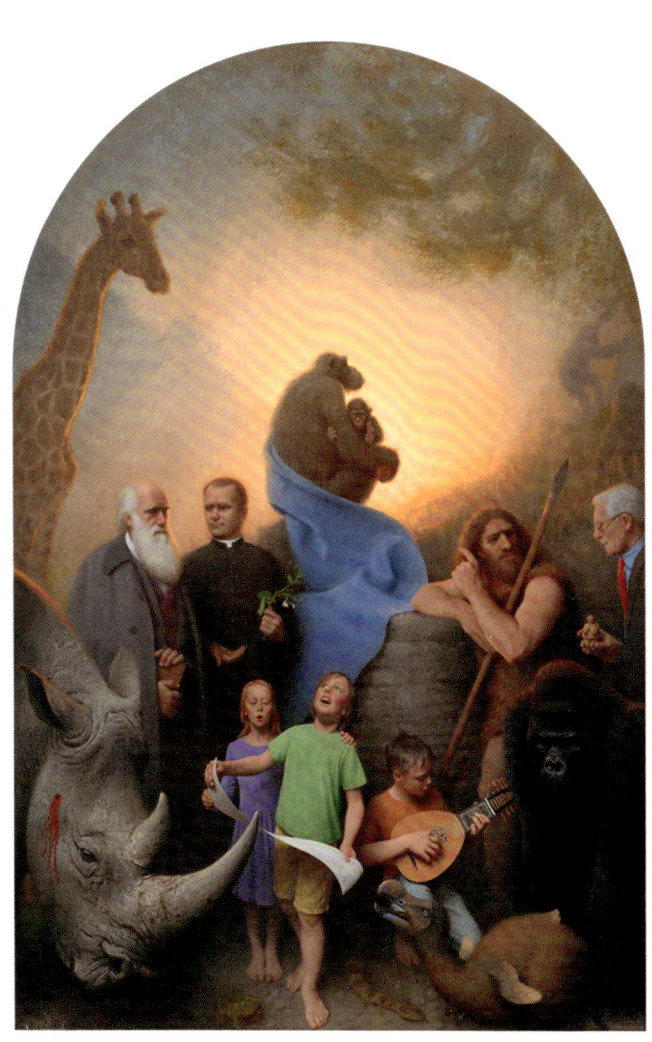

Sheepskin and Cactus
Antony Williams

Egg tempera on board
530 × 610mm

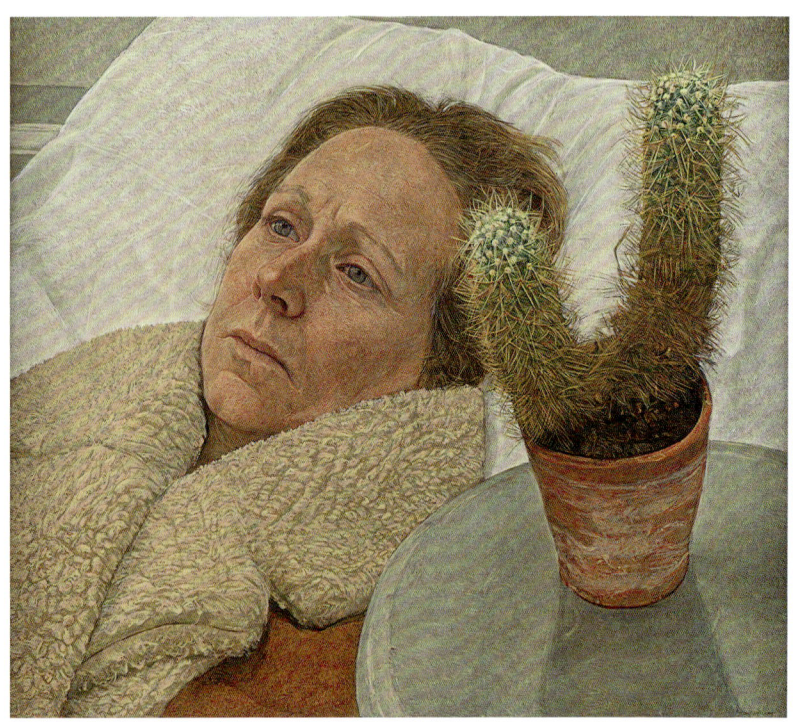

Patchwork
Paula Wilson

Oil on board
360 × 280mm

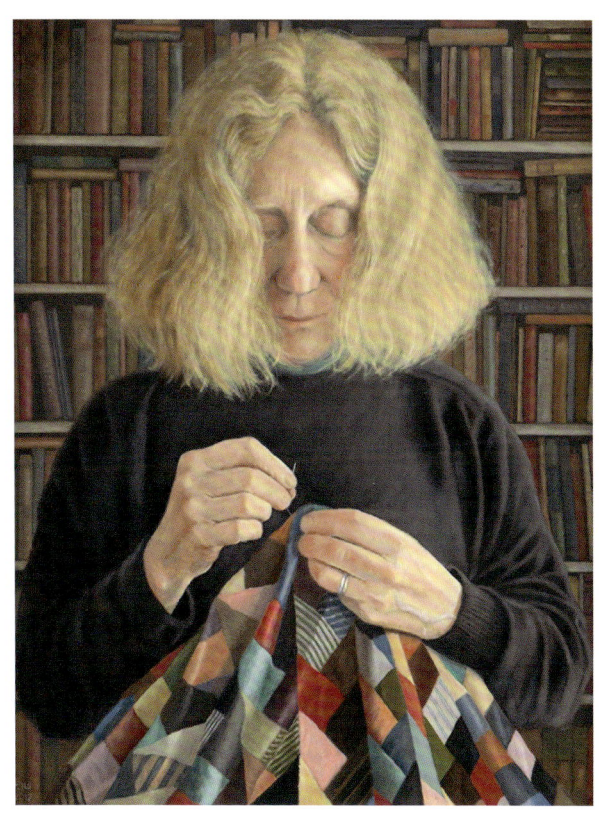

Ilea
Neale Worley

Oil on canvas
1060 × 500mm

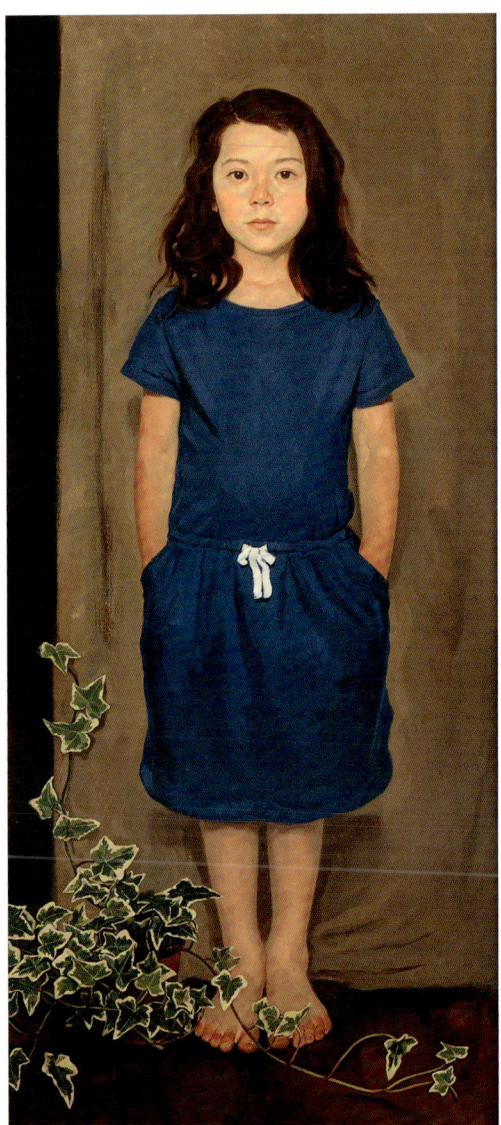

Sister
Zack Zdrale

Oil on panel
300 × 300mm

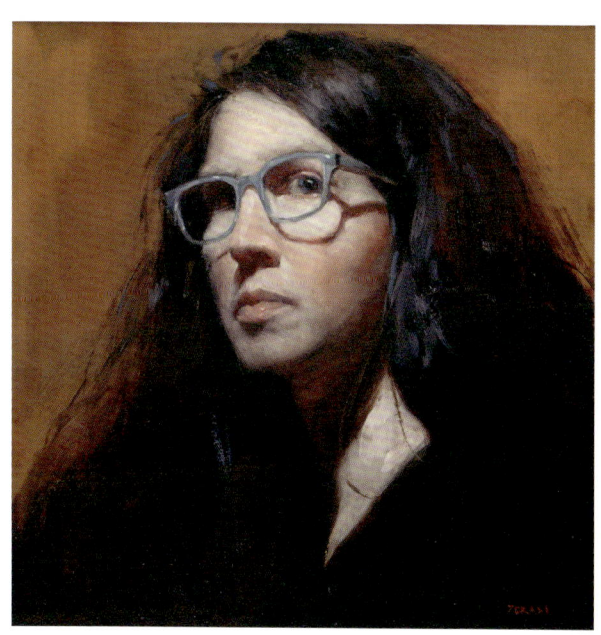

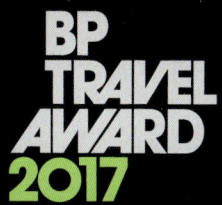

BP TRAVEL AWARD 2017

Each year exhibitors are invited to submit a proposal for the BP Travel Award. The aim of this award is to give an artist the opportunity to experience working in a different environment in Britain or abroad, and on a project related to portraiture. The artist's work is then shown as part of the following year's BP Portrait Award exhibition and tour.

THE JUDGES

Clara Drummond
Artist and winner of
2016 BP Portrait Award

Rosie Broadley
Collections Curator,
National Portrait Gallery

Des Violaris
Director, UK Arts & Culture, BP

The Prizewinner 2017
Casper White, who received £6,000 for his proposal to create works about music fans in the clubs and concert venues of Berlin and Mallorca.

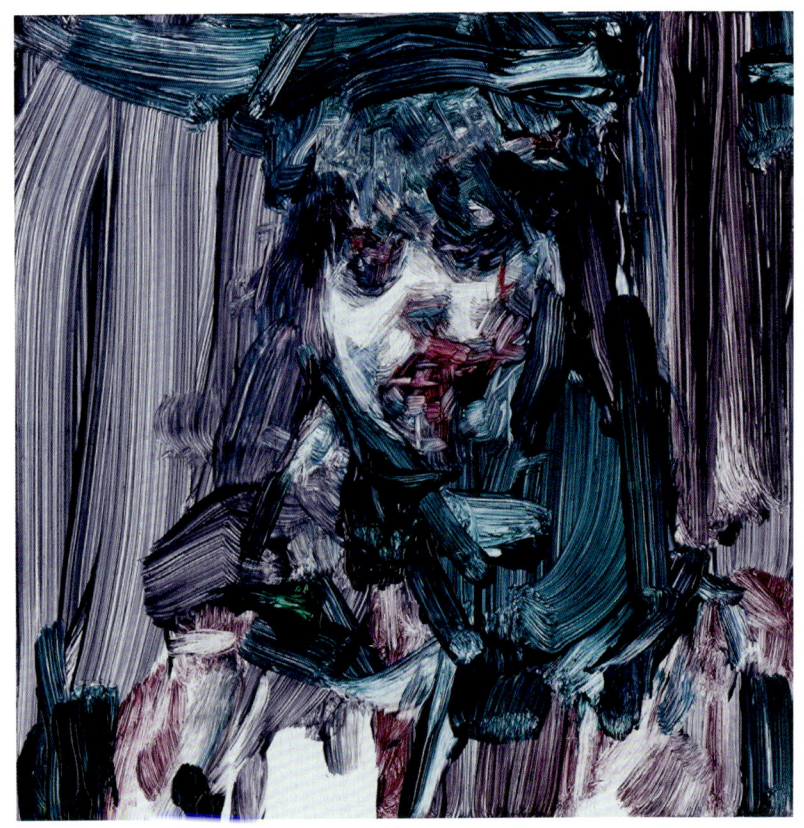

It Just Feels Gross
by Casper White, 2018
Oil on zinc, 200 x 200mm

PORTRAITS FROM THE CLUB SCENE IN EUROPE

Casper White

Casper White received the 2017 BP Travel Award after impressing the judges with his proposal to paint the portraits of young people attending clubs, concerts and gigs throughout Europe. The artist wanted to explore a youth subculture not traditionally recorded in painting: a person losing themselves dancing in a nightclub; a fan staring up at a band from the front of the crowd.

Born in the former coal-mining town of Maesteg in the South Wales Valleys, White gained a BA (Hons) in Fine Art at Cardiff School of Art and Design followed by an MA in Fine Art (Contemporary Dialogues) at the University of Wales Trinity Saint David, Lampeter. His interest in portraiture initially derived from painting family members, then developed during life drawing classes he attended on an Erasmus programme at Accademia di Belle Arti Lorenzo da Viterbo in central Italy. Aged 36, he is closely involved with an artist-led curatorial project in Cardiff called LLE, and has also had his work featured in group exhibitions in London and Manchester.

White's previous portraiture has focused on his family and his friends in the Cardiff art scene, while a recent series of oil paintings depicted young adults on their mobile phones. As an occasional musician and regular gig-goer, White saw the Travel Award as an opportunity to mine his interests in the 'unseen places and times' inhabited by youth culture, while taking a Sickert-like look at the way audience and performance coexist.

'A portrait is traditionally made of the star, the performer, but I wished to invert this, turning my focus around to the person engaged as a fan,' explains White. 'These people are fully immersed in the experience and the wider lifestyle. I hoped to capture this moment in an authentic way as I feel these people are inadequately documented, especially within portrait painting. I'm interested in the careless abandon these environments foster; the euphoria of the experience.'

To begin the project, White first travelled to Berlin and Leipzig with four of his friends, all artists or musicians, spending two weeks in Germany, experiencing the nightlife at rock concerts and techno clubs, before later visiting Mallorca where he sampled the island's club and gig cultures. 'I felt Berlin could offer a broad view of clubs and music venues mostly frequented by locals, while the Balearic Islands would give

a different angle. The islands are full of so-called super-clubs which attract people from all over Europe on what seem like modern-day pilgrimages.'

One of his earliest choices was to portray his own friends in the finished works rather than asking strangers to pose for him. 'As a studio painter the idea of having to go out and find a model is quite daunting, even in Cardiff, let alone Leipzig or Berlin,' he says. 'I did not want to approach random people in clubs, so I asked my friends to come along as my models to diffuse any sense of voyeuristic undertones.'

Deciding to paint the portraits back at his studio, White used the club nights as a recce to assemble as much information and reference material as he could. In his visits to Berlin clubs, bouncers forcefully informed him that smartphones and cameras were forbidden, leading him to experiment instead with different techniques to record the venues' mood, ambience and lighting – including using watercolours on surfaces pre-prepared with dark paint to minimise the attention he would attract in low-light environments. 'I found myself making gestural works recording colours and contrasts, and studies that conveyed atmosphere,' he explains.

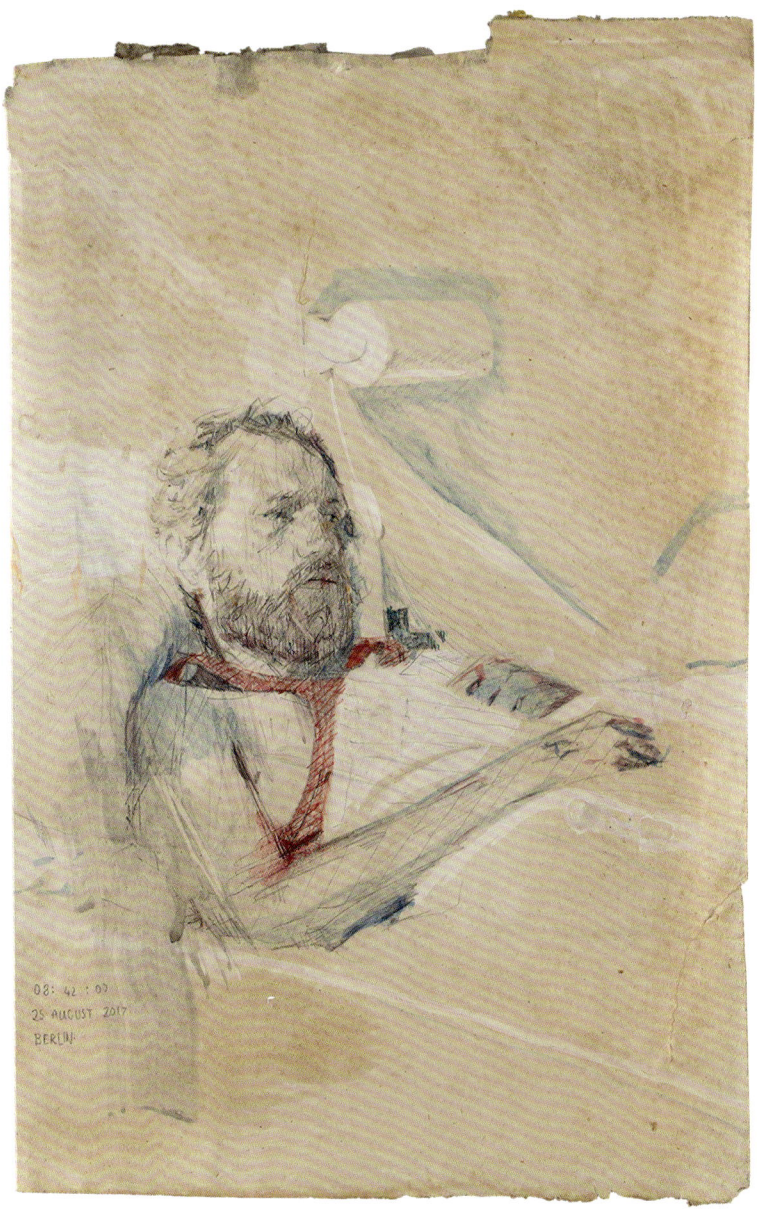

Next Day (Owain)
by Casper White, 2018
Pencil and watercolour on found paper, 250 x 160mm

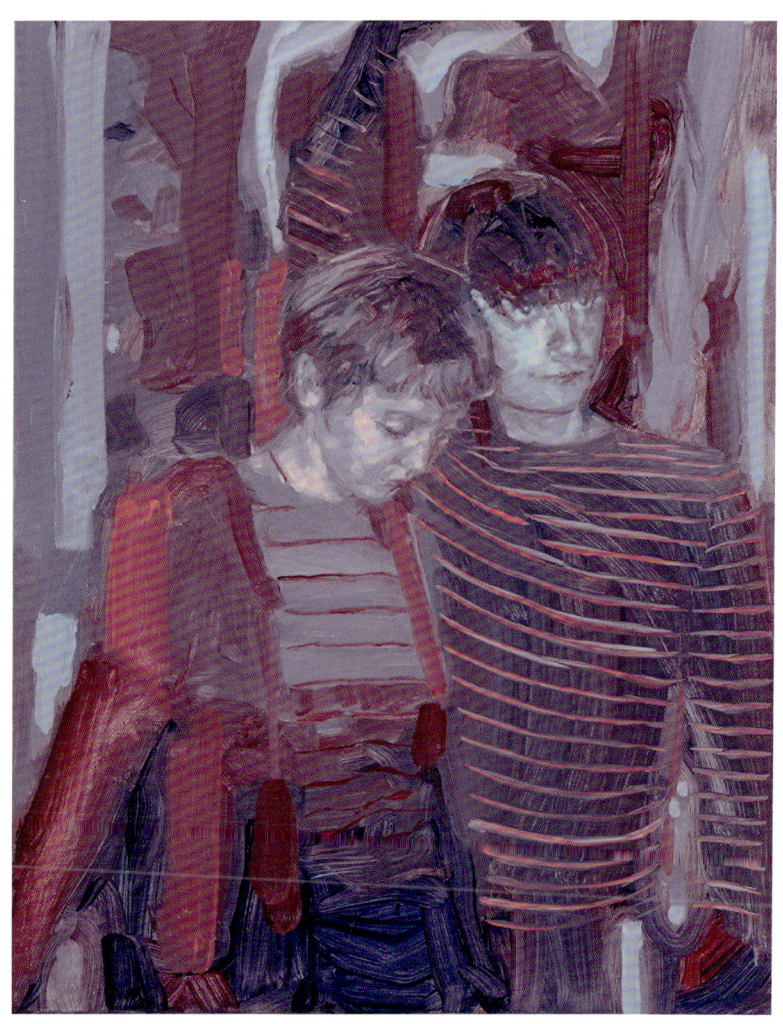

Have to Warm up to the Feel of it (Mabli and George)
by Casper White, 2018
Oil on canvas, 500 x 400mm

'These sketches in the clubs were hard-fought, but became influencers in gesture and mood when I returned to the studio.'

In order to fully capture his surroundings, White says it was also important that he immersed himself in the clubbing and bar experience: 'We were out every night. Nothing too wild, but I soon discovered that drawing, drinking and dancing is hard work and don't necessarily work well together.'

While in Germany, White also began drawing his friends during their hangovers from the night before, using various found objects, from gig flyers to old record sleeves, to use as surfaces for the works. A pencil and watercolour portrait of his musician friend Owain, entitled *Next Day*, was made on a found piece of paper after the group had been to the Pop-Kultur festival in the German capital.

'We had a great night and ended up back at our hostel,' says White. 'In the morning, people were tired, hungover and open to being drawn in this state. The portrait of Owain seems timeless; it reminds me of a Toulouse-Lautrec drawing and made me reconsider Ingres drawings I have seen. Portraying these intimate moments was one of the most exciting parts of my stay in Berlin.'

On his return to Wales, White determined to make his large-scale portraits as intimate as his pencil drawings. 'That became a focus,' he says. 'You'd expect most clubs to be a throng of people, but despite the crowds, you can still enjoy a relatively intimate space. I wanted to recreate that intimacy rather than paint big groups of people.'

White worked on the portraits while listening to various tracks he'd heard at the clubs in a bid to replicate the experience, rigging up disco lights and spotlights in his studio to re-establish the club vibe (most of the paintings' titles are taken from this music). Calling upon his fellow clubbers and friends to pose again, he initially reconsidered the sketches as oil-on-canvas paintings, including a study of friends George and Mabli entitled *Have to Warm Up to the Feel of it*.

'This painting involved using a very limited palette, mainly purples,' says White. 'In dark surroundings, the flesh can become devoid of the skin's usual tones and tints – similar to the marble of classical sculpture. In clubs,

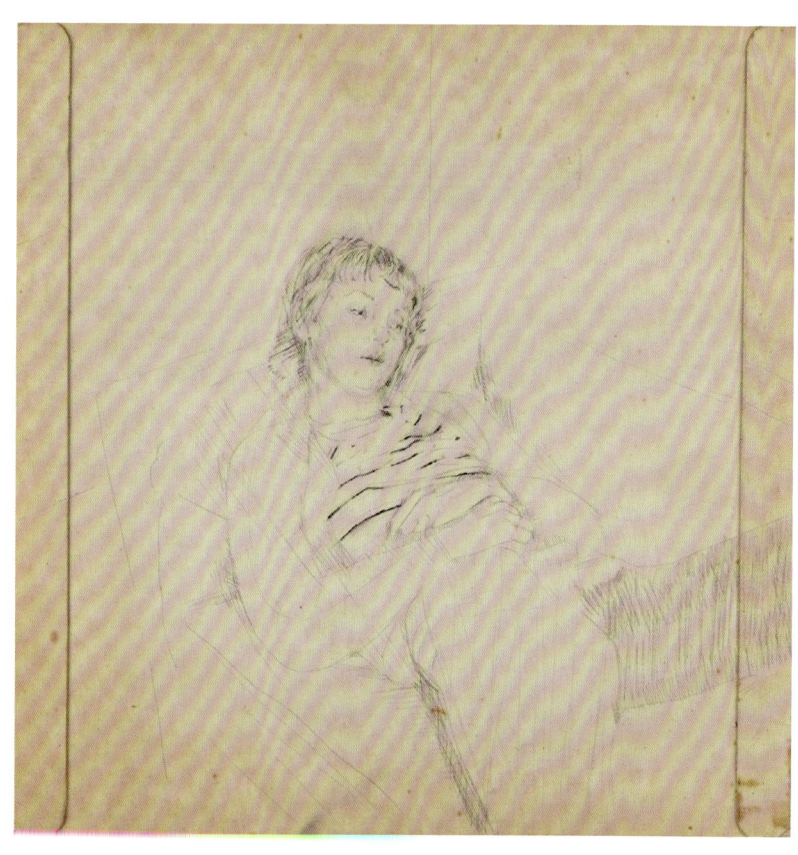

Next Day (Mabli)
by Casper White, 2018
Pencil on found record sleeve, 260 x 260mm

the light is often at such high contrast that shadow and light areas are at the very extremes visually.'

For other works, White opted for varnished stainless steel, zinc and copper surfaces, which he felt were more suited to capturing light and movement. He'd previously used zinc as the surface for his entry in the 2017 BP Portrait Award, a picture of his nephew Jack that was selected for exhibition, and he attempted to refine this technique with his new paintings.

Into a Light (Mabli) is a large-scale oil painting on stainless steel. The portrait is a build-up of marks in reds and blues, and the face contains no flesh tones. 'The stripes are, in a way, more detailed than the face,' says White. 'Stripes reappear in a lot of the work produced during this period, suggesting the body but also implying movement. Within this work, you can also see some of the gestural marks taken from the initial sketches I made in the clubs in Berlin.

'I found that when I painted on metallic surfaces, the light was reflected off areas that I left unpainted,' he adds. 'Here, the light moves across the painting, the work mutates and changes, giving an element of movement within the work. In the past, I have been interested in portraying people's features, but with this project, I have tried pushing my painting to articulate something else as well as likeness to a sitter.'

Having now finished several portraits from his time in Germany, and continuing to complete the Mallorca section, White believes the Travel Award is likely to constitute the first step in an ongoing project that examines what it is to portray people outside the constraints of a traditional sitting.

'These images portray things that are happening most weekends around the world, and I hope the viewer can find a few interesting passages of paint,' he says. 'I do not want to hang the most pristine finished work, nor the most attractive, but I hope this is an exciting collection of drawings, paintings, detritus and debris – one that is a fair record of an interesting period of research.'

Interview by Richard McClure

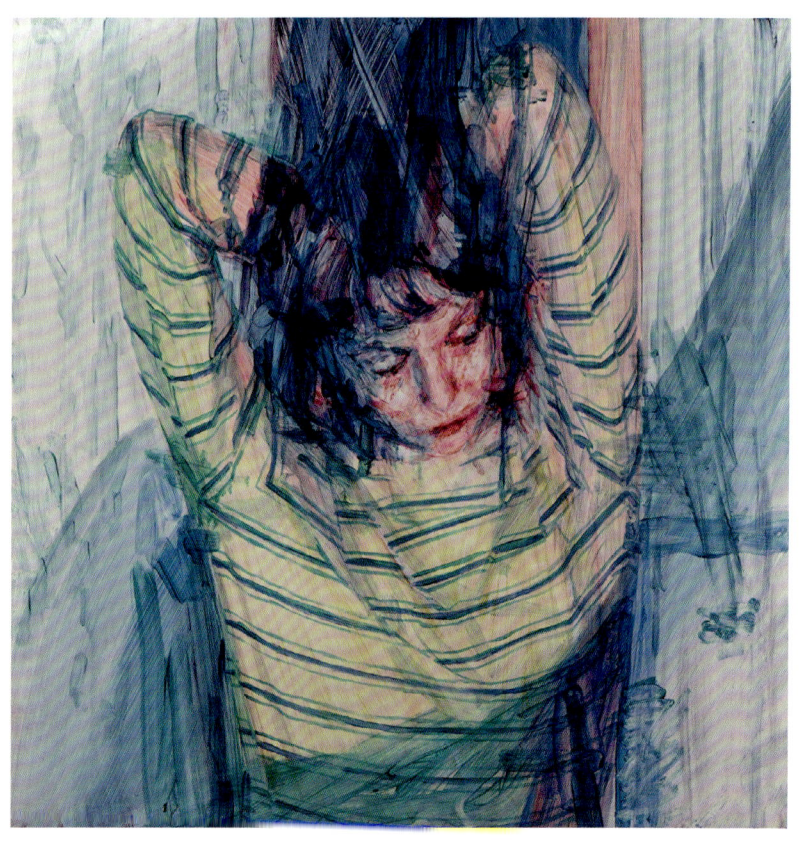

Into a Light (Mabli)
by Casper White, 2018
Stainless steel, 1250 x 1250mm

ACKNOWLEDGEMENTS

I would like to thank all the artists who decided to enter the 2018 competition. My many congratulations are offered to all the artists in the exhibition and in particular to the prizewinners, Miriam Escofet, Felicia Forte and Zhu Tongyao, and to Ania Hobson, the winner of the prize for a younger painter.

My sincerest thanks to my fellow judges: Dr Caroline Bressey, Rosie Broadley, Glenn Brown, Rosie Millard and Des Violaris. They were both insightful and observant regarding the task at hand and it was delightful to work with them all. I would also like to thank the judges of the BP Travel Award: Rosie Broadley, Clara Drummond and Des Violaris. My thanks to Rosie Broadley for her insightful essay. I am very grateful to Kara Green, Richard McClure, Christopher Tinker and Tijana Todorinovic for their editorial work, Richard Ardagh Studio for

designing the catalogue, and to Clementine Williamson for her overall management of the 2018 BP Portrait Award, ably assisted by Ulrike Wachsmann. Many other colleagues at the National Portrait Gallery have been involved in making the competition and exhibition a continued success and my thanks for their hard work go to Pim Baxter, Miranda Banfield, James Cunninghame Graham, Andrea Easey, Neil Evans, Evie Hone, Jessica Litwin, Anne McAteer, Laura McKechan, Justine McLisky, Ruth Müller-Wirth, Nicola Saunders, Jude Simmons, Alison Smith, Fiona Smith, Liz Smith, Emily Summerscale, Sarah Tinsley, Ben Weaver, Helen Whiteoak, Rosie Wilson, and Karl Lydon and the art handling team. Many thanks to The White Wall Company for their contribution to the efficient management of the selection and judging process.

Nicholas Cullinan
Director, National Portrait Gallery

INDEX